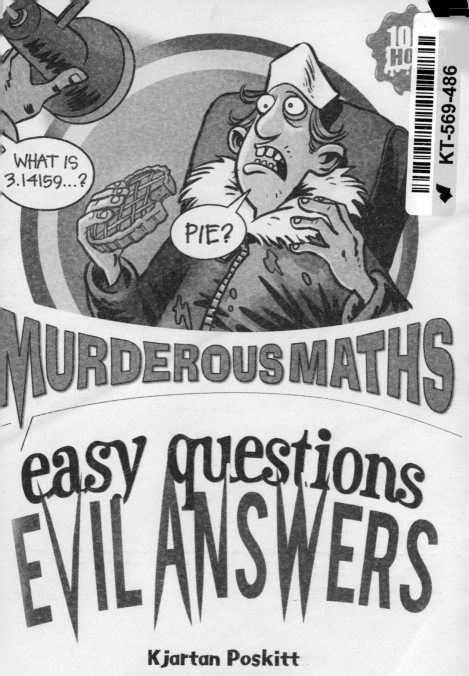

MURDEROUS MATHS

easy questions
EVIL ANSWERS

Kjartan Poskitt

illustrated by **Philip Reeve**

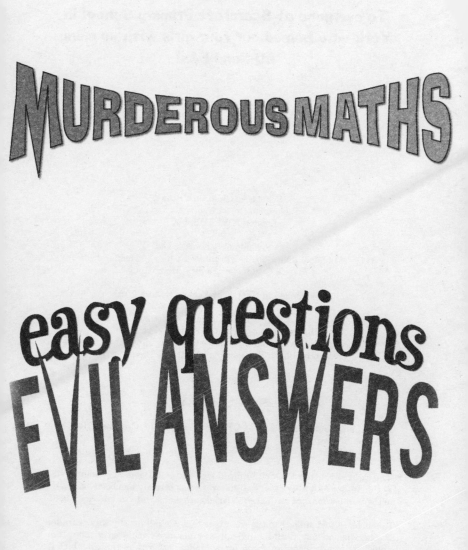

MURDEROUS MATHS

easy questions EVIL ANSWERS

To everyone at Scarcroft Primary School in York who helped our four girls with so many EQs and EAs!

Scholastic Children's Books,
Euston House, 24 Eversholt Street,
London NW1 1DB, UK

A division of Scholastic Ltd
London ~ New York ~ Toronto ~ Sydney ~ Auckland
Mexico City ~ New Delhi ~ Hong Kong

Published in the UK by Scholastic Ltd, 2010

ISBN 978 1407 11451 4

Printed and bound in the UK by CPI Group (UK) Ltd, Croydon, CR0 4YY

13

Contents

The Suggestion Box   7

Some useful stuff   13

Arithmetricks   14

The Formula Board   23

Pytho Power   25

When does 9 − 11 = 10?   31

How far away is the horizon?   37

How fast does the moon move?   42

The Great Rhun and the Box of
One Year's Delight   46

Calendar chaos!   49

What is the very smallest measurement?   58

How can you make a liar tell the truth?   64

How far does a water current make
you drift off course?   69

What is the biggest shape you
can put a fence around?   75

How many snaps does it take to
break up a chocolate bar?   78

How many different nets of
a cube are there?   81

Did Dolly diddle the dodgy diamonds?   84

Why can't you get a giant
people-eating spider?   86

What's that nasty thing in the basement?   93

How many people in the world
share your birthday?   100

The shortest link   109

A lot of hot air   113

How do you make a perfect kite
shape quickly?   117

What is the biggest number?   119

The curry burger problem   131

How high is a kite?   133

Can one giant sneeze blast
the Earth out of orbit?   137

The mysterious handcuffs   142

Some unexpectedly evil football sums   144

How much of Archimedes' bathwater
is in every glass of water you drink?   156

Goodbye!   158

The Suggestion Box

Have you got a question bothering you that seems nice and easy, and yet nobody will give you an answer? It's probably because even though the question might look easy, the answer is evil!

Don't worry. Murderous Maths takes on the questions that nobody else dares to touch, and we work out the evil answers. To start us off we got everybody we know to write their own questions on pieces of paper.

We got so many good questions it was hard to know where to start, so we put them all in a box and mixed them up, then we pulled one out to see who would go first.

Guess who won?

It's Binkie Smallbrains from Fogsworth Manor. He offered to perform an opening number to get us all in a jolly mood so we said YES. Binkie said he knew a really good tune, even though it's only six notes long. The only trouble is that he can't quite remember how it goes so he's playing around until he finds it.

You'd think if the tune is only six notes long it shouldn't take too long to find. Actually you'd be surprised. Just like a lot of normal everyday things, it gives us a rather good easy question ... with an extremely evil answer!

How many different tunes can you play on a piano?
Binkie's piano has 77 different notes on it, so this gives him lots to choose from.

If Binkie can't choose any notes, then the number of tunes he can play is zero. At least that's nice and simple.

The notes Binkie can play are G, A, B, C.

If his tune was only going to be one note long, then he only has four different choices of what to play: G, A, B or C.

If his tune had two notes in it, then the number of different tunes he can play is $4 \times 4 = 16$. (The 16 tunes are GG GA GB GC   AG AA AB AC BG BA BB BC   CG CA CB or CC.)

If Binkie plays as many as six notes, there are $4 \times 4 \times 4 \times 4 \times 4 \times 4 = 4,096$ different tunes. (We can write $4 \times 4 \times 4 \times 4 \times 4 \times 4$ as 4^6 which is going to make things a lot easier in a minute.)

9

Actually Binky can get a LOT more than just 4,096 tunes in six notes.

One of the tunes is GGAGCB which would be the tune for "Happy Birthday To You", but only if each note is the right length. For instance the two notes for "Hap-py" are both quite short, but the note for "you" is a long one.

Here are some of the most common lengths of note with their names:

WHAT THE NOTE LOOKS LIKE ON MUSIC:	♪	♩	♩	𝅗𝅥	𝅝
HOW MANY BEATS IT LASTS:	¼	½	1	2	4
NAME:	SEMI-QUAVER	QUAVER	CROTCHET	MINIM	SEMI-BREVE

(There are lots of other note lengths, such as "dotted minims" that last for 3 beats or "demisemiquavers" that last for $\frac{1}{8}$ of a beat, but this lot will do for now.)

When you see a note written on music, it tells you how long it should last and how high or low it has to be.

THIS ONE WOULD BE A VERY SHORT HIGH SQUEAK

BIP! NOTES: GG A G C B

OOOO!

HAP-PY BIRTH-DAY TO YOU

THIS ONE WOULD BE A LONG NOTE LIKE A LOW HUMMING NOISE.

When Binkie plays one note, how many different ways can he do it? Here's how to work it out:

NUMBER OF WAYS OF PLAYING ONE NOTE = NUMBER OF DIFFERENT NOTES TO CHOOSE FROM X NUMBER OF DIFFERENT NOTE LENGTHS

Binkie can choose from the notes G, A, B or C and then if he chooses one of the five common lengths, in total he has 4 × 5 = 20 ways of playing one note. So how many ways can he play six notes?

The answer is 20 × 20 × 20 × 20 ×20 × 20 (which we can write as 20^6) and this comes to ... 64,000,000 different ways. Only one of these ways will sound exactly like "Happy Birthday to You"!

(By the way – if you're learning a new instrument and can only play 4 different notes, you can play *sixty-four million* six-note tunes too! So why don't you stick your tuba out of the window right now and give your next door neighbours a concert? They'll be ever so grateful.)

If Binkie can use all 77 notes, then how many ways can he play one note? 77 × 5 = 385. How many ways can he play six notes? 385^6 = 3,256,599,688,890,625.

And that's if he only pokes at the notes one at time with his pencil. Suppose Binkie starts to play chords that use four notes at once. How many ways can he play his first chord?

When Binkie plays chords, the sums get so evil that this book could burst into flames so we'll just get a rough idea. So long as Binkie doesn't put both his hands right up at the top end, or right down at the bottom, he'll have about 40 choices for his highest note and 40 choices for his lowest note. We'll also assume he plays two notes with each hand and each hand can stretch across a maximum of 12 notes. This gives him 12 choices for each of the two notes in the middle of the chord. He can also choose one of the five note lengths, so just to play his first chord he has $40 \times 40 \times 12 \times 12 \times 5 = 1,152,000$ choices.

Are you ready for your first really evil answer? Here it comes!

If Binkie plays six chords and each chord has four notes in it, the number of different tunes he can make is about:

$$1,152,000^6 =$$
$$2,337,302,235,907,620,864,000,000,000,000,000,000$$

And how many of those tunes will sound nice?

Some useful stuff

Although there are millions of questions in maths, you can answer most of them with one or more of the following things:

- Arithmetricks
- Formulas
- π
- Pytho Power
- Devious thinking

There are also a few optional extras that will help:

- RANDOM HAIR
- AN ORANGE NYLON SHIRT
- HALF A CHEESE AND CHUTNEY SANDWICH IN YOUR POCKET THAT'S BEEN THROUGH THE WASH
- UNDONE SHOELACES

We'll work through the list and see how each of these things can help us.

Arithmetricks

We've already sorted out Binkie's piano with a bit of arithmetic. Even though we only did a spot of multiplying, it gave us some really evil answers. It's amazing what you can do with just + − × and ÷ and if you want to check how they all work, you'll find them explained in *Murderous Maths: Awesome Arithmetricks*. However, we've saved a few special arithmetricks for this book!

Can I divide everybody in the world into football teams?

That depends on how many people there are. Let's say that there are exactly 6,794,703,256. As there are 11 players on a football team, you need to know if this number divides by 11. Here's the trick:

You go along the number putting in − and + signs alternately. You get:

$$6 - 7 + 9 - 4 + 7 - 0 + 3 - 2 + 5 - 6$$

Now you work it out. You might find it easier to separate all the + and − bits first. Remember that each sign sticks with the number that comes after it.

$$6 + 9 + 7 + 3 + 5 \qquad -7 - 4 - 0 - 2 - 6$$

If you combine all the + bits and then all the − bits you get 30 − 19 = 11.

If the answer is 0 or divides exactly by 11, then the big number will divide by 11 too! The answer here is 11, so obviously it divides by 11. That means 6,794,703,256 will also divide by 11.

Even better news! 6,794,703,256 is an even number so it also divides by 2. That means you can have an even number of teams, so everybody can play at once. But just a minute ... what's this?

Oh no! One extra person has turned up. Actually maybe that's not such a bad thing, because we ought to have at least one referee. Give that baby a whistle and a bit of respect.

What is the easiest times table to learn?

This is one of the questions that our Pure Mathematicians have been investigating down in the Murderous Maths research department.

Obviously there's a bit of disagreement here, but you can always trust our Pure Mathematicians to discuss these matters in a responsible and intelligent way.

Sorry about that. It looks like you'll just have to make your own mind up whether the easiest times table is 0, 1, 10 or 11 ... or could it be the 1089 times table?

$1 \times 1089 = 1\,0\,8\,9$
$2 \times 1089 = 2\,1\,7\,8$
$3 \times 1089 = 3\,2\,6\,7$
$4 \times 1089 = 4\,3\,5\,6$
$5 \times 1089 = 5\,4\,4\,5$
$6 \times 1089 = 6\,5\,3\,4$
$7 \times 1089 = 7\,6\,2\,3$
$8 \times 1089 = 8\,7\,1\,2$
$9 \times 1089 = 9\,8\,0\,1$

It seems like it should be evil until you look down the answers. The numbers in the first column go 1, 2, 3, 4, 5, 6, 7, 8, 9. Now look at the other columns! The really odd one is 9 × 1089. It turns backwards!

Although the 1089 times table is easy to learn, it's a bit useless unless you happen to be buying lots of things that cost £10.89. However there is one times table that isn't too tricky and it's the only one you'll ever need! All will be revealed with our next question...

Is there a times table that will multiply ANY two numbers?

Yes! You only need the 2 times table and a trick that's known as **Russian Peasant Multiplication**. Suppose you want to multiply 43 × 87.

- Write the numbers at the top of two columns.

- Keep dividing the number on the left by 2 and write the answers underneath. Ignore any remainders. Put * by any even numbers.

43	87
21	174
*10	348
5	696
*2	1,392
1	2,784
	= 3,741

- Keep multiplying the number on the right by 2 and write the answers underneath.

- Cross out any lines with *.

- Add up the remaining numbers on the right.

- Ta-dah!

What's a square root?

It's the opposite of "squared". (It's worth knowing about square roots because they are the secret to using the awesome Pytho Power coming soon.)

You can work out 3 squared by making a square with dots.

Total number of dots = 3 x 3 = 9

If a number is multiplied by itself, that's called "squared" and we usually mark it with a little ^{2}. Therefore "three squared" is $3^2 = 3 \times 3 = 9$.

We can also put this: $\sqrt{9} = 3$. The funny sign means "square root" and $\sqrt{9}$ is asking "what number multiplied by itself makes 9?"

Easy square roots: If a number is called a square, then that means it has a whole number for a square root. For instance 25 and 64 are both squares, because $\sqrt{25} = 5$ and $\sqrt{64} = 8$.

Evil square roots: Most numbers are not squares and this makes their square roots very evil. Luckily calculators usually have a button marked $\sqrt{}$ so if you need to work out the square root of 17 you just push 17 and then $\sqrt{}$ which gives you the answer 4·1231056… and this decimal will keep on going past the end of the screen and out of the door and down the road and catch the bus to Doncaster if you let it.

Hello, what's this? Somebody has put an extra question in.

How are you supposed to get $\sqrt{3806.89}$ WITHOUT a calculator, eh? Har har!

Oh dear. One way of doing it is to guess and then test your answer. To work out $\sqrt{3806{\cdot}89}$ you could guess the square root is 60 then you work out $60^2 = 3600$. That's a bit small so you try a bigger guess. How about 62? $62^2 = 3844$ so it's a bit too big. So then you try 61^2, and then you might *yawn* try $61{\cdot}5^2$ and then *big YAWN* you might try $61{\cdot}8^2$ and then you might ... *zzz* snore *ZZZZZ* ... eh? Whazzat?

It's no good. If you want to get the right answer without guessing then you have to use one of the mysterious dark powers that schools are terrified of teaching these days. Maybe your granny can remember things like "how to turn your brother into a mushroom" or "how to make snakes come out of the air vents" but that stuff's easy. Square roots are so evil that we'll need to summon Thag our Mathemagician.

IF YOU'RE A WIZARD AT SUMS, HERE'S SOME REAL MAGIC FOR YOU!

You start by writing down the number you want to square root, then put a line over it so your answer can go on top. You then draw a thin line up through the decimal point, and this shows where the decimal point will come in the answer. Next you put in another thin line to split your number into pairs of digits.

$\sqrt{38\,{:}\,06\,{\cdot}\,89}$ When you get round to writing your answer in, you'll just put one digit in each gap.

To start with you look at the first pair of digits and see what is the highest square number you can take away from it.

Here the first digits are 38, so the highest square number we could take away is 36, which is 6 × 6. This gives us 6 as our first digit in the answer and we put that on the top line. We also put 36 underneath the 38. We then subtract 38 − 36 to see the remainder = 2.

Now comes the magic bit that nobody can ever remember.

- You bring down the next pair of digits and tag them on to the end of the remainder.

- You get the answer you've worked out so far and double it. (So 6 × 2 = 12) You then write it down but you leave one extra space for a *new mystery digit*. Oo-er! We'll call it *.

- You now need to work out the new mystery digit. Here we're going to end up multiplying the number 12* by *. We have to choose * to be the biggest number we can so that 12* × * does not go over 206. If we make * into 1, then the sum is 121 × 1 = 121. This is less than 206, but is 1 the best we can do? Suppose we made * into 2? The sum would be 122 × 2 = 244 which is bigger than 206 so that's no good. Therefore * = 1. Phew!

We put the mystery digit 1 in the answer. We also multiply it by 121 and put the answer under the 206. Then we subtract to get the remainder of 85.

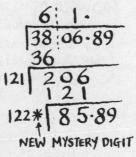

$$\begin{array}{r}
6 \quad 1 \quad \\
\sqrt{38\ 06\ 89}
\end{array}$$

MYSTERY DIGIT GOES IN THE ANSWER

36

$$121\ \overline{)\ 2\ 0\ 6}$$
$$\underline{1\ 2\ 1}$$
$$85$$

121 × 1 = 121 WHICH GOES UNDER HERE

SUBTRACT 206–121 TO GET REMAINDER

IT'S TIME TO DO THAT MAGIC BIT ALL OVER AGAIN!

You'll see we brought down the next two digits 89 and fixed them onto the 85 at the bottom. We take the answer we've worked out so far and double it (so that's 61 × 2 = 122) and write it down leaving a gap for a new mystery digit. We then work out the biggest number that * can be if 122* × * isn't going to go over 8589. It turns out that 1227 × 7 = 8589 exactly!

$$\begin{array}{r}
6 \quad 1 \cdot \\
\sqrt{38\ 06 \cdot 89}
\end{array}$$

36

$$121\ \overline{)\ 2\ 0\ 6}$$
$$\underline{1\ 2\ 1}$$
$$122*\ \overline{)\ 8\ 5 \cdot 89}$$

NEW MYSTERY DIGIT

We bang it in and by the time we've finished we find we've got no remainder. This means that $\sqrt{3806\cdot89} = 61\cdot7$.

Here's what the finished sum looks like.

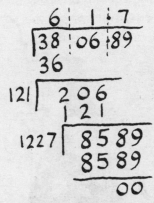

We've been dead lucky here because we got an exact answer with no remainder so we can stop. If we hadn't been so lucky then we'd continue by bringing down two more zeros to sit by the remainder and then we'd do the magic bit that nobody can ever remember again. If you're loving it you can you keep on bringing down zeros and doing the magic bit over and over again, and make a decimal that goes on for ever.

So is Thag loving it?

HEY GRANNY, HOW CAN I MAKE SNAKES COME OUT OF THE AIR VENTS?

The Formula Board

Lots of easy questions involve flat areas or lumps, so we always keep this handy list of formulas pinned up on our notice board.

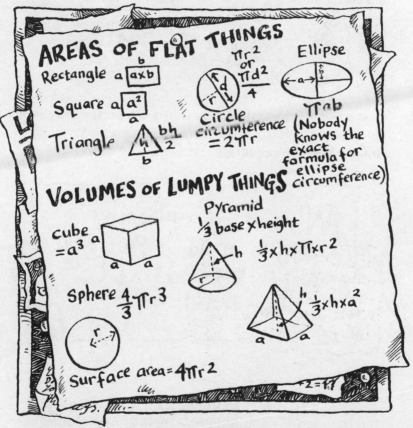

AREAS OF FLAT THINGS

Rectangle a $a \times b$

Square a a^2

Triangle $\frac{bh}{2}$

Circle πr^2 or $\frac{\pi d^2}{4}$

circumference $= 2\pi r$

Ellipse πab (Nobody knows the exact formula for ellipse circumference)

VOLUMES OF LUMPY THINGS

cube $= a^3$

Pyramid $\frac{1}{3}$ base $\times$ height $\frac{1}{3} \times h \times \pi \times r^2$

$\frac{1}{3} \times h \times a^2$

Sphere $\frac{4}{3}\pi r^3$

Surface area $= 4\pi r^2$

You'll notice that the formulas that involve anything round such as a circle or sphere have a funny little sign in them. If you're not sure what π is then this one's for you...

What is π?

If you get any circle and measure the circumference, then divide it by the diameter you always get this answer: 3·14159265358979323846264433832795…

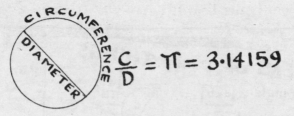

$$\frac{C}{D} = \pi = 3.14159$$

It's one of those decimals that goes on for ever, so to save writing it out there's a little sign for it: π. It's a Greek letter called "pi".

> What is the millionth digit of π? Bet you don't know that! Har, har!

We do actually. The millionth digit of π is a 1 and for that matter the billionth digit is a 9. But why would anybody want to know that?

Pytho Power

What is Pythagoras' Theorem?

It's an evil rule that involves any triangle with a right angle. Thanks to Pytho Power we can answer thousands of very awkward questions including:

- How long is a helter-skelter?
- Can you wire up an alien power system?
- How high is a kite?
- How far away is the horizon?
- What are the chances of a football bouncing off the goalpost into the goal?

These questions are all coming up later on, so first we'll see what Pythagoras' theorem says and why it works.

In a right-angled triangle:

If you measure the two short sides and square the results, they add up to the long side squared.

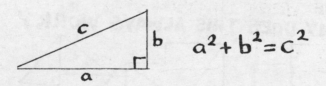

$$a^2 + b^2 = c^2$$

Why does it work?

The Greek mathematician Pythagoras was the first person to prove this rule over 2,500 years ago, but since then there have been more than 300 other proofs which use drawings, algebra, numbers, circles, tins of paint, cheese and just about anything else you can think of.

PAINT? CHEESE?
OI, SHOW SOME RESPECT!

Here's a really nice proof that doesn't involve any sums, you just stare at a few pictures.

PYTHAGORAS' THEOREM

GET ANY RIGHT-ANGLED TRIANGLE AND DRAW SQUARES ON THE SIDES.

PYTHAGORAS PROVED THAT THE SQUARES ON THE TWO SMALL SIDES ALWAYS HAVE TO ADD UP TO MAKE THE SQUARE ON THE BIG SIDE.

WHY DOES THIS ALWAYS WORK?

THIS SHAPE CAN BE MADE BY PUTTING THE TWO SMALLER SQUARES TOGETHER.

YOU CAN CUT TWO EXACT COPIES OF THE TRIANGLE FROM THIS SHAPE.

NOW REARRANGE THE PIECES. THIS SQUARE IS EXACTLY THE SAME SIZE AS THE BIG SQUARE. THEREFORE THE TWO SMALL SQUARES = THE BIG SQUARE!

OOH, THAT'S A NICE ONE!

How long is the slide on a helter-skelter?

It seems like a simple question, but to answer it we need Pythagoras and also a bit of devious thinking.

When you slide down a helter-skelter you're moving in two directions at once. You're going from the top to the bottom, and you're going round and round it.

Let's say the helter-skelter is 12 metres high, it has a circumference of 10 metres and the slide goes around 3 times. How do we work it out?

It's time for a bit of *devious thinking.*

Imagine unrolling the helter-skelter so that the slide is a straight line. You get a triangle with the height up the side, and the distance you travel around the helter-skelter along the bottom. Now we can see what's going on!

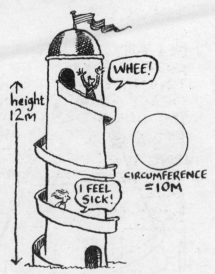

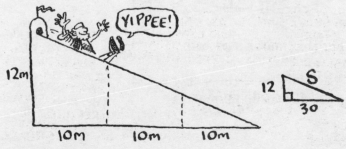

27

You can work out exactly how far you go using Pythagoras! If s is the length of the slide then:

$$s^2 = 12^2 + 30^2 = 144 + 900 = 1044$$
$$s = \sqrt{1044} = 32 \cdot 31 \text{ metres}$$

What if the helter-skelter is cone-shaped?

Most helter-skelters are thinner at the top, but that's not a big problem. You just need to know the circumference of the helter-skelter halfway up.

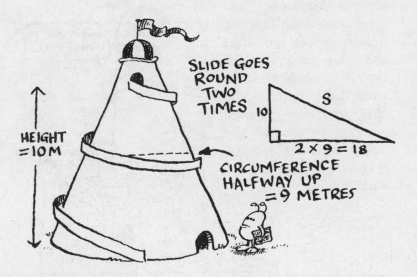

SLIDE GOES ROUND TWO TIMES

HEIGHT = 10M

10

S

$2 \times 9 = 18$

CIRCUMFERENCE HALFWAY UP = 9 METRES

For this helter-skelter:

$$s^2 = 10^2 + 18^2 = 100 + 324 = 424$$
$$s = \sqrt{424} = 20 \cdot 59 \text{ metres}$$

When do you need an orange nylon shirt, random hair, undone shoelaces and half a cheese and chutney sandwich in your pocket that's been through the wash?

There are some questions in maths that can't be answered using formulas or arithmetic. You have to have the very special sort of brain that usually comes with the above items. In other words you have to be an utterly nutty Pure Mathematician. Here's the sort of question we mean:

What is the smallest number of squares a big square can be divided into?

If all the squares have to be different then this easy question has a truly evil answer! It's just the sort of pointless thing that drives our Pure Mathematicians even nuttier than ever. They would happily spend years working it out, but fortunately for them a Dutch genius called Arie Duijvestijn has saved them the trouble.

The answer is 21 squares, which goes to show that evil answers don't have to involve massive big numbers or lots of fiddly sums. It did involve some devious thinking though!

His final answer involved dividing up this big square that measured 112 cm along each side. The side lengths of the smaller squares are all marked in.

Awesome.

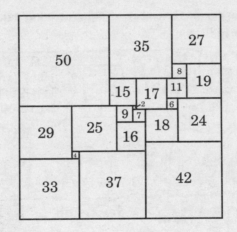

When does 9 − 11 = 10?

Adding and subtracting are not always as simple as you might think, as this report from police files shows.

Place: Somewhere in the Pacific Ocean
Date: 31 August 1929
Time: 9:05 am

The sun blazed down as the waves gradually nudged the little white boat towards the silver beach. A seagull hovered overhead to see if anyone was on board, but all it could make out was a massive load of sheets, towels and odd socks heaped across the deck. The seagull was puzzled. The engine was chugging away but there didn't seem to be anyone in the tiny little steering cabin. The seagull swooped down and landed on the prow just as the boat ground to a halt on the sand.

"Whassat?" said a sleepy voice. A corner of a sheet flopped over and a head in a Homburg hat popped out. Blade Boccelli rubbed his eyes then looked around. "Hey, we're on land! Jimmy, Porky, the rest of you, wake up! It's the morning and we made it."

The sheets and towels all started twisting and heaving as six more men stopped snoring and spluttering, untangled themselves and sat up. They were all wearing crumpled suits and squashed hats.

"Gee!" they all said. "Have we really done it, Blade?"

"We sure have," said Blade proudly. "We are the first guys ever to escape from Sharkfin Island!" He scrambled to his feet and looked up and down the deserted beach. "Can you see any prison walls? Any barbed wire?"

"No," agreed Weasel, the smallest man. "But I thought you said we were going to land at Skipporridge?"

"Yeah, where's the docks?" said Half-Smile Gabrianni. "And the buildings, and the lights?"

"And the restaurants?" said the largest man. Porky Boccelli's stomach was rumbling like a tractor engine. "I need to eat, and soon!"

"Listen, you guys," said Blade. "Skipporridge has to be here somewhere. Look at the map. The autosteer kept the boat pointing due east all night."

"So maybe we haven't been sailing long enough?" said Weasel.

"This boat goes at eight miles an hour, and we had to do eighty miles. How long would that take, Numbers?" asked Blade.

32

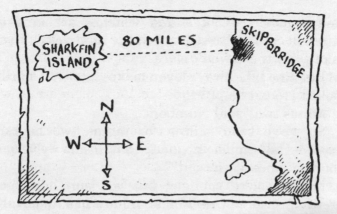

The thinnest man thought for a second. "Eighty miles divided by eight miles per hour, that makes ten hours, Blade."

"OK," said Blade. "Hey, Chainsaw Charlie, how long we been sailing for?"

The tallest man checked his watch and then thought very hard. "I reckon it was … er … two hours."

"Two hours?" they all gasped.

"Oh boy," muttered Blade. "The only one of us with a watch and the only one who can't tell the time."

"Hang on, Chainsaw," said Half-Smile Gabrianni. "We were sailing all night. How can that be two hours?"

"Yeah, we waited till it was dark, sneaked into the laundry boat and set off at eleven o'clock," said Weasel.

"And it's just past nine o'clock now," said Chainsaw. "So eleven take away nine makes two. Like I said, it was two hours."

"That's not how it works,"

said Numbers. "Clocks and watches are kind of different. You got to start with the nine o'clock then take away the eleven o'clock."

"But nine take away eleven makes ... er..." Charlie looked around helplessly.

"Minus two," said Numbers.

"So we've been sailing for minus two hours?" gasped Half-Smile. "So does that mean we've got younger since we set out?"

"Maybe you're younger, but you sure ain't got prettier," sneered One-Finger Jimmy. In a fury, Half-Smile grabbed the first thing that came to hand and hit Jimmy over the head with all his might. Jimmy fell to the deck clutching his face until he realized that he'd just been clobbered by a grubby vest and it didn't hurt at all.

"Cool it, you guys," said Blade. "If we want to know where we are, we need to figure out what's going on! How can a night be minus two hours long?"

The answer is that the dials on clocks and watches only use the numbers from 1–12. When the hands go round, after they go past 12 they start again at 1. Suppose clocks started at 00:00 on 1st January in the year AD 0 but when the hours got past 12 they kept on counting 13, 14, 15 and so on going up for ever. What would Chainsaw's watch say at 9:05 am on 31st August 1929? The answer is ... five minutes past sixteen million, nine hundred and six thousand, three hundred and five. Chainsaw's watch would need to be very big to fit all the numbers on.

That's why we tell the time with **clock arithmetic** which means when you get past 12, you just go back to 1 again. If you need to subtract one time from another, it's often best to start at the earlier time and see how many hours and minutes you need to add on. Here's how long Blade and the gang were really on the boat:

START — ADD 1 HOUR — ADD 9 HOURS — ADD 5 MINUTES

TIME IS 11:00 — MOVE ON TO 12:00 — MOVE ON TO 9:00 — MOVE ON THE EXTRA FIVE MINUTES

TOTAL TIME = 10 HOURS + 5 MINUTES

Luckily for Blade, they had another way of seeing how long they had been sailing for. A huge rumbling noise echoed along the beach.

"Gee, was that your guts singing, Porky?" said Weasel.

"I can't help it," said Porky. "The last thing I ate was one little bread roll just before we got on the boat."

"One little bread roll plus one giant meat loaf," said Half-Smile.

"That meat loaf was just to give it a bit of flavouring," said Porky. "And flavouring doesn't count."

"I recognize your hungry gut noises," said Blade. He put his ear to the big man's stomach. "Now there should be a little hiss and then some bubbles ... yup, there they go! That was the ten-hour-and-ten-minute rumble."

"You can tell the time from his guts?" gasped Weasel in amazement.

"Sure I can," said Blade, poking his brother's midriff with his finger. "And his guts don't get fooled by fancy clocks and watches' numbers. They know darn well that nothing's passed through them for over ten hours."

"So we were on the boat sailing east for ten hours at eight miles an hour, which means we went eighty miles," said Numbers.

"So where's Skipporridge?" demanded Weasel.

They all stared out across the sea at the empty horizon.

"I guess it must be somewhere out over there," said Numbers.

"So how far away can we see?" asked Weasel.

"That's a very good question," sighed Blade.

To be continued…

How far away is the horizon?

If you are standing on a beach with the edge of the sea just touching your toes then for a quick answer check this table:

HOW FAR YOUR EYES ARE FROM THE GROUND	YOUR SITUATION	DISTANCE TO THE HORIZON
1.2 m	SMALL PERSON	3.91km (2.42 MILES)
1.5 m	MEDIUM PERSON	4.37km (2.71 MILES)
1.8 m	TALL PERSON	4.78km (2.96 MILES)
5 m	YOU'RE A GIRAFFE	8 km (ABOUT 5 MILES)
30 m	YOU'RE TIED TO A KITE	19.5km (ABOUT 12 MILES)

Obviously tall people can see further than small people, so if you're not tall you can always build a sandcastle and stand on it. A sandcastle that's 30 cm high will let you see more than 400 metres further away.

NOTE: IN THESE DIAGRAMS THE SIZE OF THE EARTH HAS BEEN REDUCED.

NORMAL PERSON HORIZON = 4.5km

LIGHTHOUSE KEEPER CAN SEE FURTHER

IF YOU STAND IN A HOLE WITH YOUR EYES AT GROUND LEVEL, HORIZON DISTANCE = 0KM

How did we work it out?

We used the special Murderous Maths horizon formula:

$$d = 3.57 \times \sqrt{H}$$

where d = distance to the horizon in km and H = height of your eyes above the ground in metres. So if your eyes are 1·5 metres above the ground, the distance to the horizon is $3.57 \times \sqrt{1.5} = 3.57 \times 1.225 = 4.37$ km.

(Some people use the formula $d = \sqrt{13H}$ which is easier to remember but the answers are about 1% too big.)

Hey you cheats! Why should anybody trust your Murderous Maths horizon formula? I bet you just grabbed any old numbers and stuck them in. So there!

These notes are getting irritating now. We did NOT just grab any old numbers! To prove it we'll work out the horizon distance with Pythagoras' Theorem which we saw back on page 25. The first thing we need is a right-angled triangle and this calls for some devious thinking.

Imagine two lines drawn from the centre of the Earth, one to your feet and the other to the horizon. These lines will both be the radius of the Earth, which is about 6,370 km. Now imagine a line from your eyes to the horizon. This line is the distance we want to find out, and rather helpfully it makes a tangent with the curve of the Earth.

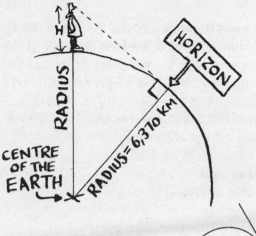

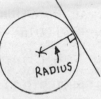

A tangent is a line that only touches a circle once. The angle between a tangent and the radius it touches is always 90°.

You can see from the diagram we've got a right-angled triangle. If we take away the Earth it looks a bit clearer:

r = the radius of the Earth, which is about 6,370 km

H = the height of your eyes above the Earth = 1·5 metres

d = the distance to the horizon

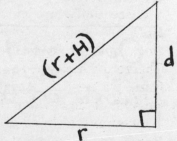

Of course in real life H is tiny compared to r so the shape of this triangle should look more like this one:

...but it would be even longer and pointier.

First we need to work out the length of the $(r + H)$ side. We know $H = 1\cdot5$ metres, but as the other distances are in km, so we need H in km too. We divide 1·5 metres by 1,000 to give $H = 0\cdot0015$ km. Now we know that $(r + H) = 6370\cdot0015$ km. That little extra 0·0015 km on the end might look tiny, but it makes all the difference!

Pythagoras says:
$$6370^2 + d^2 = 6370\cdot0015^2$$

We can move this round to get:
$$d^2 = 6370\cdot0015^2 - 6370^2$$

Now we do the sums:
$$d^2 = 40576919\cdot11 - 40576900 = 19\cdot11$$

So finally $d = \sqrt{19\cdot11} = 4\cdot37$ km. That's the same answer that we got with our formula, so the formula WORKS, OK?

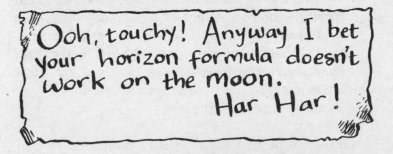

Oh, yes, it does. We just need to make one little change...

How far away is the horizon on the moon?

The radius of the moon is only 1,737 km, so the moon horizon formula has a different number in it:

$$d \text{ (for the moon)} = 1 \cdot 86 \times \sqrt{H}$$

Suppose the moon was a perfect sphere without any mountains, craters, abandoned alien caravans or talking trees, then if your eyes were 1·5 m above the surface, the distance to the horizon works out to be 2·28 km (or 1·41 miles).

So even though you're still the same height, the moon horizon is about half the distance away compared to Earth. One good thing about being on the moon is that gravity is about $\frac{1}{6}$ of Earth's gravity, so if you like you could jump up to maybe a height of 3 metres. In this case your total eye height would be 3 + 1·5 = 4·5 metres. If you plonk this into the formula you'll find that when you jump up you can see nearly 4 km. How lovely, so don't forget to take your camera.

How fast does the moon move?

This is a real trick question. When you watch the moon, it seems to rise up, move across the sky, and then set on the other side. If it's a full moon, it takes about two minutes to move its own width across the sky.

If it was going at this speed, it would go round the Earth about once every 24 hours, but of course the moon isn't moving as fast as that. It only seems that fast because the Earth is spinning round. If the Earth was glued down so it couldn't move or spin at all, then the moon would only get right round us once every 27·32 days. This is called one **sidereal month**. To do this it travels about 2,415,000 km at an average speed of 1·023 km per second.

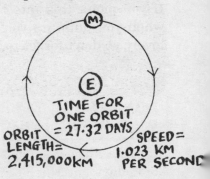

How often do we get a full moon?

Although the moon goes round the Earth every 27·32 days, the Earth is going round the Sun at the same time. This makes things a bit trickier!

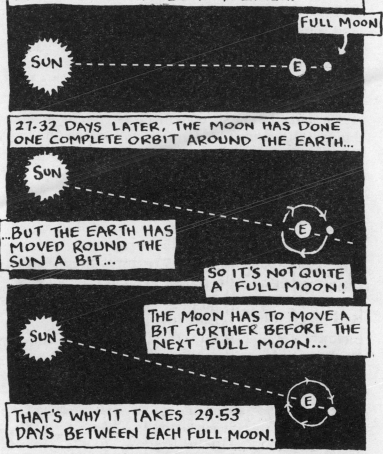

So the answer is that we get a full moon every 29·53 days and this is called a **synodic month**.

How often is Once in a Blue Moon?

A blue moon is when a full moon occurs twice in the same calendar month. For instance there's a full moon on 2nd August 2012, and there will be a second full moon on 31st August 2012. The second one is the "blue" moon.

As there are about 29·5 days between full moons and the average month length is about 30·5 days, blue moons only happen about once in every 30 months but not in a regular pattern. Occasionally we get two blue moons in the same year. The last double blue moons happened in January and March 1999 and the next ones will be January and March 2018, and then January and March 2037.

Will we ever see a Green Moon?

Let's hope not. The only green moon we know about has just been invaded by the Evil Gollarks from the planet Zog. They've called it Lunagoll, and we suspect they're planning to cause trouble.

At any time exactly half the moon will be lit up and the other half will be dark, so *where should the solar panels go?* And a solar panel won't work if it's half in light and half in shade.

You can try this yourself. Instead of having a moon half lit up and half dark, imagine you're going to slice an orange exactly in half. Before you slice it, can you put three dots on the orange, so that it doesn't matter which direction you slice the orange, there will be at least one dot on each half?

The answer is that it's impossible! The best you can do is put your three dots around a circumference of the orange. When you come to cut the orange in half, the three dots will all be chopped in half. It's the same with the Gollark solar panels. The best they can do is put them around the equator of the moon, but if it spins the wrong way, all three panels will only be half lit and so won't work.

The Great Rhun and the Box of One Year's Delight

MANY TALES ARE TOLD OF THE GREAT RHUN OF JEPATTI. ALTHOUGH HE WAS FAMED FOR HIS RICHES, HIS GREAT WEALTH WAS SURPASSED BY HIS EVEN GREATER CUNNING!

BEWARE: LOW-FLYING CARPETS

One morning there did arrive in the palace of the Great Rhun a travelling merchant by name of Hotgud the Hawker. As ever he wore his coat of 1,000 pockets.

"What trifle do you hope to sell me today?" demanded the Great Rhun. "I already have at least one of everything that has ever been made."

"But see this, oh Your Greatness," spake Hotgud the Hawker, and he pulled a small box from pocket number 672. The Great Rhun reached forward to raise the lid, but Hotgud pulled it away. "Be warned!

This is the mystic Box of One Year's Delight. Before it is opened you must know of its conditions."

"Conditions?" asked the Rhun.

"The price is 1,000 ftarrps," said Hotgud the Hawker, "and then the box shall be yours. While it is in your keeping, flowers shall spring from your footprints, your shadow will glitter in the darkness, your voice will sing so sweetly that it will cause even the mountain wolves to smile."

The Great Rhun raised an impressed eyebrow. "Then I shall have it."

"But heed this! Before the end of one year, you must sell the box again, and the price must be lower than that which you paid."

"What if I don't sell?"

"Then the curse of eternity shall smite you and your household. Demons shall devour your horses, a plague shall ravage your family and your teeth shall turn to slugs."

The Great Rhun scratched his Great Chin with his Great Fingernail. He liked the idea of a year's delight, but the curse didn't sound much fun. And yet, to avoid the curse, all he had to do was sell the box for less than 1,000 ftarrps?

"I know what Your Greatness is thinking," said Hotgud. "But the box must be sold for a whole number of ftarrps, no fractions. And you MUST warn the buyer that he too must sell before his year of delight has passed."

The Great Rhun sighed. He had always longed for flowery footprints, a glittery shadow and a girly voice, and yet with a wave of his hand he dismissed the Hawker.

Why did the Rhun not buy the box?

Answer:
Anybody who buys the box has to be sure of selling it on for less than was paid. Therefore nobody will buy the box for 1 ffarrp. This means that if someone bought it for 2 ffarrps, they could never sell it. Therefore nobody will buy the box for 2 ffarrps, and so nobody who bought the box for 3 ffarrps would be able to sell it. The Great Rhun realized that this argument goes on for ever, and so nobody should ever buy the mystic box at any price!

Calendar chaos!

Why are there 14 different calendars?

So how long will Pongo have to wait until he can use the same calendar again?

Most years have 365 days in them. If it was only 364 days, they would divide by 7 to give exactly 52 weeks in every year and 1st January would always be on the same day of the week. However 365 ÷ 7 gives us 52 weeks with one extra day left over. This extra day means that if 1st January is on a Monday in a normal year, next year it will move along one day to Tuesday. That's why there are seven different versions of the normal calendar, each of them starting on a different day of the week.

What makes it even more complicated is that every fourth year has an extra day added: 29th February. This is called a leap year because if 1st January is a Monday then the next 1st January will leap a day and be a Wednesday. There are also seven different versions of leap year calendars which start on different days of the week, therefore in total there are 14 different calendars.

When can I use my old calendar again?

Every 28 years you'll find you use each of the seven normal calendars three times, but you'll only use each of the seven leap year calendars once. (The only time this rule changes is when we start a new century, but we'll worry about that later.)

Why do we bother with leap years?

The Earth goes right around the sun about once in every $365\frac{1}{4}$ days. If our calendars had 365 days in every year then after about 700 years, our dates would be $700 \times \frac{1}{4} = 175$ days ahead of the Earth's position in the sky. This means we'd be getting July weather in January, which would make things very confusing for snowmen.

(This joke won't make much sense if you're in Australia because you normally get summer in January and instead you'd be getting winter.)

That's why back in 46 BC the Roman Emperor Julius Caesar made everybody use the "Julian Calendar" which adds an extra day every fourth year, and that kept everything running fairly smoothly.

Unfortunately the Earth doesn't take exactly $365\frac{1}{4}$ days to go round the sun. It's more like 365 days, 5 hours and 49 minutes. In 1582 the Italian astronomer Aloysius Lilius calculated that we can adjust for these 11 missing minutes by missing out three 29th Februarys in every 400 years. He said that if the year divided by 100 you shouldn't have a leap year, unless the year divides by 400 in which case you DO have a leap year. So 2100 won't be a leap year but 2000 was. This new calendar is known as the Gregorian calendar after Pope Gregory XIII who tried to get everyone to use it. Poor old Aloysius who did all the hard work didn't get his name used for the calendar, but instead they named the "Lilius Crater" on the moon after him.

Was there ever a 30ᵗʰ February?

Yes! Some countries did what the Pope said very quickly, and that involved missing 10 days out of the calendar because there had been too many 29ᵗʰ Februarys. In 1582 Italy, Spain and Portugal skipped from 4ᵗʰ October to 15ᵗʰ October, so if your birthday was on 5ᵗʰ October it was your tough luck. France and other Catholic countries caught up soon afterwards.

A lot of other countries didn't take up the Gregorian calendar until years later, so for a long time people were using different dates for the same day. Britain didn't change to the new calendar until 1752 and by then they had to miss out 11 days so they went to bed on 2ⁿᵈ September and woke up on 14ᵗʰ September. However the prize for being the craziest calendar chaos country goes to ... *Sweden!*

HEY KING! MOST OF EUROPE USES THE GREGORIAN CALENDAR NOW. WE NEED TO MISS 10 DAYS OUT SO OUR DATES CAN BE THE SAME AS THEIRS.

MISS 10 DAYS? THAT SOUNDS A BIT DODGY...

King Charles XII of Sweden and also Finland (1697-1718)

Everything you've just seen is true. Mad, but true. There have been other 30th Februarys in history as other countries experimented with making all the months the same length, but Sweden's single random 30th February is the funniest, so here's a special message for our Swedish friends: *Vi älskar det!*

How often is there a fifth Sunday in February?

Sunday, 29th February only occurs once every 28 years. This happens when you're using a leap year calendar which starts with 1st January on a Thursday. The last time was in 2004 and the next time will in 2032.

What does the Swedish sentence "Vi älskar det" mean?

Oh go on then, we'll put you out of your misery. It means "We love it".

How often does Friday 13th occur?

The simple sum goes like this: there are 7 days in the week, so the 13th of the month has a $\frac{1}{7}$ chance of falling on a Friday. In a period of 28 years you'll get 48 Friday 13[th]s. The way that calendars work out, there has to be at least one Friday 13th in every year and there can't be more than three.

Actually Friday 13th is slightly spookier than that. If you want to be really accurate, you have to allow for the fact that the Gregorian calendar misses out 3 leap years in every 400 years. This means that the total number of days in 400 years (which includes 97 29th Februarys) is $400 \times 365 + 97 = 146,097$. This number divides exactly by 7 which means that the weekdays aren't random at all, they are in a set pattern. In 400 years there are $400 \times 12 = 4,800$ months and it turns out that:

684 months have the 13th day on a Saturday
687 months have the 13th day on a Sunday
685 months have the 13th day on a Monday
685 months have the 13th day on a Tuesday
687 months have the 13th day on a Wednesday
684 months have the 13th day on a Thursday...
...*and **688** months have the 13th day on a Friday!*

Therefore the 13th is very slightly more likely to be on a Friday than any other day of the week!

Why do people think that Friday 13th is unlucky?

Fear of Friday 13th has only been going for about 200 years. It's called *paraskavedekatriaphobia* and nobody is quite sure how it got started. It's probably because in olden times, a lot of people thought Fridays were unlucky (e.g. some sailors would not set sail on a Friday), and 13 has always been considered unlucky, so Friday 13th is just a combination of the two. The odd thing is that there are slightly fewer road accidents and crimes on Friday 13th because people are more careful!

One good story about why Friday 13th is unlucky stars the ancient Norse Goddess Frigga which is where the name "Friday" came from. When the Christians took over, they called her a witch and banished her to live on a mountain top. To get her revenge, on every Friday she used to meet up with 11 witches and the devil himself (which makes a group of 13) to plan all the evil things that would happen in the next week.

How can I work out what weekday my birthday will be on this year?

Working out weekdays can be really tedious. You end up counting lots of sevens, and then trying to remember which months have 31 days, but a genius called John Conway devised a peculiar short cut.

There are ten key dates in a year that always fall on the same day of the week, and they are not hard to remember! They are:

4/4, 6/6, 8/8, 10/10, 12/12 and 9/5, 5/9 and 7/11, 11/7

In other words: 4th April, 6th June, 8th August, 10th October, 12th December, 9th May, 5th September, 11th July and 7th November.

The final key date is *the last day of February*

which could be either 28th February or 29th February if it's a leap year.

So suppose today is 15th May and it's a Tuesday. What day of the week will 18th November be? The nearest key date to 15th May is 9th May, so we need to find out what that is. If we start on 15th May and subtract 7 we can see that 8th May will also be a Tuesday. This means that our key date 9th May is a Wednesday. Therefore 7th November will also be a Wednesday. Add 7 to find 14th November is a Wednesday, and then count along so that 15th is Thurday, 16th is Friday, 17th is Saturday and 18th is a Sunday. With practice it just takes a few seconds!

If you need to find a weekday for March, it's handy to *remember* it's the same as *November*. (So 7/11 is the same weekday as 7/3.)

For January or February, you need to think a bit harder. Just remember that 28th February and 31st January (31/1) and 3rd January (3/1) are always the same weekday.

How can I remember which months have 31 days?

Close your fists and put your hands together. Imagine the months written out on your knuckles and the gaps between them. The months that land on the knuckles have 31 days!

MONTHS WITH 31 DAYS SIT ON TOP OF YOUR KNUCKLES

What is the very smallest measurement?

If you start with one metre and keep dividing it by 1,000, there are a whole set of different names for the tiny little lengths you get. When you write the lengths as decimals you end up with bucket-loads of zeros, unless you know the short cut which uses *negative powers*. Here's how it works:

10^3 means $\frac{1}{10^3}$ which is $\frac{1}{10 \times 10 \times 10}$ which makes $\frac{1}{1,000}$ or 0·001

Name	How to write it	Decimal fraction	Power	Approximate length
metre	1 m	1	1	As long as a belt
millimetre	1 mm	0·001	10^{-3}	As thick as a fingernail
micrometre	1 μm	0·000001	10^{-6}	Bacteria are a few μm long
nanometre	1 nm	0·000000001	10^{-9}	A virus is usually 10–300 nm across
picometre	1 pm	There were so many zeros in this section that they got bored of being jammed up together so they dug a hole and escaped. WE'RE FREE!	10^{-12}	The smallest atom diameter is about 50 pm
femtometre	1 fm		10^{-15}	These measurements might seem silly but one of them is an answer later in the book!
attometre	1 am		10^{-18}	
zeptometre	1 zm		10^{-21}	
yoctometre	1 ym		10^{-24}	

If you think our printing machine went a bit wonky when it did the micrometre sign, it's supposed to be the Greek letter μ which is called "mu". So the printing machine is right after all, so there.

Yocto comes from the Greek word "octo" which means eight. If you divide one metre by 1,000 and keep doing it for eight times, you get a yoctometre. When you've got it, be careful not to lose it because they're very small.

If you happen to be doing a spot of spectroscopy* you might come across an *angstrom* which is 10^{-10} m, and therefore 10 angstroms = 1 nm.

*That's when you're trying to find out what a mystery chemical is by shining a light on it and seeing exactly what colours it absorbs or reflects. Here are a few examples to get you started:

WHITE = CHEESE

ORANGE = DIFFERENT CHEESE

GREEN WITH BLUE BITS = MOULDY CHEESE

...and what is the very biggest measurement?

This time we'll start with one metre and keep multiplying by 1,000.

Name	How to write it	Number	Power	Approximate length
metre	1 m	1	1	A tall person's leg
kilometre	1 km	1,000	10^3	Three times round the football pitch
megametre	1 Mm	1,000,000	10^6	London to Edinburgh and back again
gigametre	1 Gm	1,000,000,000	10^9	5 times round the equator and then to the moon and back
terametre	1 Tm	Whoops! Look where the escaping zeros have ended up...	10^{12}	The distance the Earth travels every year to go right round the sun
petametre	1 Pm	1,000,000,000,000 1,000,000,000,000,000 1,000,000,000,000,000,000	10^{15}	9·5 petametres = 1 LIGHT YEAR
exametre	1 Em	1,000,000,000,000,000,000,000	10^{18}	How far Veronica Gumfloss would run if Pongo McWhiffy tried to kiss her
zettametre	1 Zm	0 0 0 0 ARGH! THERE'S EVEN MORE OF US! 0 0 0 0 0	10^{21}	
yottametre	1 Ym	0 0 0 0 1,000,000,000,000,000,000,000,000	10^{24}	

How big is the universe?
1,000 yottametres.

Actually we don't know for certain. 1,000 Ym is only a rough guess of how far it looks from one edge to the other, but...

- maybe that's just as far as we can see. The universe could be a lot bigger but our telescopes can't see any further because they have reached the **cosmic light horizon**. Wahey! It's a bit like when you look out to sea, you can't see beyond the horizon because the Earth is curved. When telescopes stare into the sky there could be a limit to how far they can see because space might be curved. This is tricky stuff and can easily damage your brain so let's move on.
- some people think that the universe is getting bigger all the time. In fact the edges could be moving away from us at the speed of light which would make them invisible to us. But then if we can't see the edges, how do we know they're moving? Eek! Time to move on again.
- some people think the universe hasn't got any edges. It just goes on for ever.

The bit of universe we can see is called the **observable universe** and if it really is about 1,000 Ym, that's 1,000,000,000,000,000,000,000,000,000 metres. You might think this is pretty big, but here's the scary bit – later on you're going to see something that will make the universe look tiny!

How can you remember what a light year is?

It's the distance that light can travel in one year. If you're using metres to measure how far away stars and other galaxies are, you'd soon get clogged up with zeros or little twiddly powers of 10, so light years make things easier.

- 1 light year = 9,500,000,000,000,000 metres

There's a simple way to remember how many metres there are in a light year. It starts with 95 followed by 14 zeros. This is useful because $9 + 5 = 14$.

If you want to make it into kilometres you knock off three zeros.

- 1 light year = 9,500,000,000,000 km.

And then if you want to convert the kilometres into miles you just turn the 9 and the 5 around.

- 1 light year = 5,900,000,000,000 miles

Another way of remembering a light year is to think it is just under ten trillion kilometres. The nearest star to us (apart from the Sun) is Proxima Centauri and it's 4·2 light years away. This is about 40,000,000,000,000 km (or *forty million million* km or *forty trillion* km).

What's the furthest thing you can see with your eyes?

It's the Andromeda Galaxy which is 2,500,000 light years away. You need a very dark, clear night, and it looks like a tiny white smudge in the sky. If you think it's a bit boring, don't write to it and complain. You're looking at how it appeared 2,500,000 years ago because that's how long it took the light from the galaxy to get to you. For all we know it could have started flashing in groovy colours this week but it'll be another 2,500,000 years before we see it.

What's really scary is that if anybody on the Andromeda Galaxy is looking at us right now, all they'll see are a few ape creatures in Africa just starting to walk upright. Their front feet would be evolving into hands and the very latest gadget would be sharp pieces of stone to help them chop up their dinner. That's what we were like 2,500,000 years ago!

I DON'T LIKE THE LOOK OF THEM...

How can you make a liar tell the truth?

One day Urgum the Axeman was passing by the Tower of Troonott when a voice called out.

"Urgum! Help, you have to rescue me!"

Urgum looked up and saw his friend Thag the Mathemagician peering out of a high window. He pulled out his massive axe and shouted back, "Don't worry Thag, I'm coming in!"

"No, stop!" shouted Thag. "Watch out for the guards!"

Urgum looked at the two little guards who were standing in front of two doors into the tower. "Ha!" he scoffed. "They don't scare me!"

"But you have to ask them which door to come through! One door is safe but the other one drops you into a black hole full of long spikes covered in boiling hot poison."

"That's no problem!" said Urgum and he pointed at one of the doors. "Is this door safe?" he demanded and then he added a "GRRRR!" to make himself look extra scary.

"Yes," said one.

"No," said the other.

"What's going on?" gasped Urgum.

Thag shouted down from above. "One guard always tells the truth, and the other one always lies!"

"Oh really?" said Urgum waving his axe nastily. "So who's telling the truth?"

"Me!" they both said pointing at themselves.

"Bah!" said Urgum. "OK, which one of you is the liar?"

"He is," they both said pointing at each other.

"Oh no!" said Urgum. "How do I tell which door is safe?"

"There's only one thing to do," shouted Thag. "Choose one of the doors, and pick one of the guards, then ask him the magic question: *would the other guard describe this door as safe or unsafe?*"

Here's how the magic question works:

If the answer is "safe" then that's the booby-trapped door.

If the answer is "unsafe" then that's the safe door!

The magic question cleverly combines what both guards would say. As one guard says the truth and the other tells a lie, the answer has to be a lie. It's a bit like $(+1) \times (-1) = (-1)$

Urgum doesn't know which door he's chosen to ask about and he doesn't know which guard he's speaking to. This leads to four possiblities, but it doesn't matter which, the answer is always a lie.

Soon Urgum was inside the Tower and had run up the steps where he found a small door. When he turned the handle he found it was locked, but that wasn't going to stop Urgum the Axeman. One hefty whack with his axe smashed it into matches. "Out you come, Thag!" said Urgum.

"Do you mind?" said a lady's voice as a cloud of steam drifted out. "I'm having a bath."

"Ooops, sorry!" said Urgum blushing furiously and covering his eyes.

"Is that you, Urgum?" came the Mathemagician's voice from further down the passageway. "I'm in here."

Urgum ran along and found a second door bolted on the outside. In a flash he opened it up and was pleased to see Thag waiting for him.

"Let's go!" said Thag heading back the way Urgum had come.

"Er ... not that way," said Urgum who was still blushing. "Let's see if there's some other stairs." Sure enough they found a second staircase leading down to a different part of the tower. At the bottom were two more doors.

"One leads out and the other one is booby-trapped again!" said Thag.

"But which is safe?" asked Urgum. He didn't want to land on any poisoned spikes, or even worse, he didn't want to go barging into another bathroom.

Just then another Troonott guard came along. "Quick, grab him," said Thag. "Then we'll ask him about the doors."

"Are you a liar?" Urgum asked the grabbed guard.

"No," said the guard.

"Phew," said Urgum. "At least that makes things easy!"

"No it doesn't," said Thag. "He could be a liar who's lying."

"Let's ask him your magic question again."

Thag shook his head. "That won't work, because it needs two guards. But I've got another magic question that should work."

Can YOU see what Urgum should ask?

Answer:
Urgum has to choose one of the doors then this is what he asks the guard: *"If I asked you if this door was safe, would you say yes?"*

It doesn't matter if the guard tells the truth or lies, Urgum will get the right answer!

If the guard tells the truth he'll give the right answer anyway.

If the guard is a liar, this is a double question so his two lies will cancel out. The two questions are "Is this door safe?" and "did you just say yes?"

If the door is safe, then the liar would have said "no" to the first question. But then for the second question "Did you say yes?" The liar will lie and say "yes."

If the door is unsafe, then the liar would have said "yes" to the first question. But then for the second question "Did you say yes?" The liar will say "no."

How far does a water current make you drift off course?

Place: Somewhere in the Pacific Ocean
Date: 31 August 1929
Time: 10:20 am

There was a roar, a cough and a splutter as the boat's engine started up then died again. "It's no good, Blade," shouted Half-Smile from the cabin. "I think we're out of gas."

The other six men standing on the beach looked around helplessly.

"Now what do we do?" asked Weasel. "We're stuck in this place, and we don't even know where this place is."

Blade looked around in despair. It was the strangest place he'd ever been. There were no signs, no buildings, not even street lights. There was just a beach that stretched round in a big curved bay then came to an end at a high cliff. "Maybe if one of you was to climb up there, you'd see something?"

"I'll go," said One-Finger Jimmy. "I've done loads of climbing."

"Yeah, but your climbing is going up drainpipes when you're trying to break into places," said Weasel.

"So I'll find a drainpipe," said Jimmy. "There's got to be drainpipes. I've never been to a place that doesn't have drainpipes."

69

The men all nodded in agreement. Everywhere had to have drainpipes. As Jimmy set off, Half-Smile called out from the boat and waved a piece of paper. "Hey guys, look what I've found in the locker!"

"Is it something to eat?" asked Porky hopefully.

"No, it's a current map."

"Oh goody!" smiled Porky. "Is that like a treasure map, only there's no treasure, instead there's currants? I love currants. I could eat a whole ton of currants."

"It's not that kind of currant, you big dope," said Half-Smile as he splashed his way ashore. "It shows how the water current flows. Maybe we can work out where we are."

"You guys go ahead," said Porky. "I've got to get some food before I fade away." The big man waddled off towards the trees at the back of the beach.

"What are you expecting from this dump?" Chainsaw called after him. "A few nuts? Maybe some bugs?"

"I don't know," came the sad reply. "But there must be something."

The others crowded round Half-Smile to see what he'd found.

"This explains a lot," said Blade. "At the same time

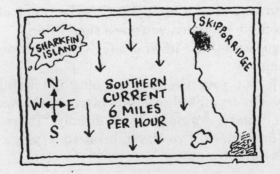

as we were heading east to Skipporridge, the water was moving us south."

"This map's no good," said Weasel. "Where's the big red dot?"

"What big red dot?"

"The big red dot that says 'You are here'. The maps stuck up in the middle of towns always have a big red dot. Why can't all maps be like that?"

"He's got a point," said Blade. "I can see Sharkfin Island. We know we sailed 80 miles to Skipporridge, but how far south did the current take us?"

If there had been no current we know that the boat would have travelled in a straight line going east for eighty miles. We can show this on the map with an arrow that's the right length. (An arrow that shows distance and direction like this is called a **vector**.)

At the same time that the boat's engine was pushing it east, the current was pushing the boat south. We know the boat was on the move for 10 hours, so how far south did the current push it? As the current speed is 6 miles per hour, the distance = 6 miles per hour × 10 hours = 60 miles. We can show this with another arrow on the map.

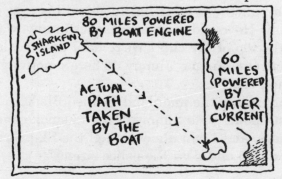

These two arrows show what the boat's path would have been if it had travelled the two distances one after the other. However, the boat was travelling in both directions at the same time, and we can find out where the boat really went by drawing one more line to complete the triangle.

Oh yes we can ... thanks to Pytho Power! If we look at the map we get a right-angled triangle.

The boat distance = $\sqrt{80^2 + 60^2}$ = $\sqrt{6400 + 3600}$ = $\sqrt{10000}$ = 100 miles

A voice came echoing down the beach. Blade looked up and pulled down his hat to shield his eyes from the sun. He could just about see Jimmy waving from the top of the cliff. "We're on a desert island," shouted One-Finger Jimmy. "There's nothing but bays and beaches."

"Can you see the mainland?" called Blade.

"Just about," said Jimmy. "There's smoke, factory chimneys, and I can almost smell the Skipporridge waste dump and hear the police sirens."

"So how are we going to get over there?" asked Weasel.

"Are you nuts?" asked Blade. "We got sun, we got sea, we got sand. People pay big money to come to a place like this and we got it for free! I'm in no hurry to go."

"But how can we survive here?" asked Weasel. "There isn't even a hot dog stand."

Just then a fabulous smell came wafting over from the back of the beach. They all ran up to find Porky sitting on a low rock by a cave entrance.

"Gee, I was just expecting nuts and bugs," said Chainsaw.

"You can have those for dessert if you like," grinned Porky. "Meanwhile you'll have to make do with this."

A small fire was crackling away, and hanging over it was a long metal boat spike that was stuck through a dozen fat fish. Warming up beside them was a bucket of coconut and banana sauce, and neatly arranged on a selection of flat stones were a mass of chopped peppers and limes.

"This is better than eating in Luigi's Diner!" said Chainsaw Charlie. "Where did you find all this stuff?"

"This island's bursting with it," said Porky.

"That cave sure looks cosy," said Half-Smile. "We could get the sheets off the laundry boat and sleep in there."

"Then tomorrow we could go fishing," said Weasel. "Or we could paddle or build sandcastles."

"Oh boy!" said Chainsaw. "That beats robbing banks and hijacking mail trains."

"And I'll make a turtle stew," said Porky.

"Mmmmmmm!" said everybody.

"That's settled then," said Blade. "Hands up who wants to stay?"

All their hands went up.

Soon they were all lying back on the sand, surrounded by fish bones and feeling full. Blade was studying the map, staring at the little island.

"What a great place to be!" he said. "But I can't make out what it's called. The printing is tiny."

"Pass it here," said Half-Smile pulling a really thick pair of spectacles out of his pocket and putting them on. "I've got great eyes."

"I believe you," said Blade. "If you can see through those things then your eyes have *got* to be good."

Half-Smile was holding the map right up against his nose. "Oh no!" he gasped in horror. "It can't be!"

"What's the matter?" asked Blade. "Can't you read it?"

"Of course I can read it," Half-Smile ripped off his spectacles and looked around in a panic. "We've got to get off this island, and fast!"

To be continued...

What is the biggest shape you can put a fence around?

This is one of those questions where you might think you know the answer, but be careful! Sometimes it isn't quite so obvious as it seems. Let's check on the Gollarks who are still trying to make a base on Lunagoll, but now they've got some unexpected visitors.

There are lots of different shapes the Ploogs could mark out with their 100 metres of fence. If they were going for a rectangle shape here are some of the options:

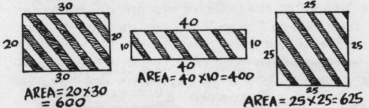

30

20

30

AREA = 20 × 30 = 600

40

10

40

AREA = 40 × 10 = 400

25

25

25

25

AREA = 25 × 25 = 625

Obviously the square has the biggest area, but there is an even better option.

For once the Gollarks are right.

What area of circle can you make with 100 metres of fence?

We need to use two π formulas for this one.

AREA = πr²
CIRCUMFERENCE = 2πr
(π = 3·14159...)

We know the circumference of the circle is 100 metres, so first we work out the radius r.

$$100 = 2\pi r$$

If we divide both sides of this equation by 2π and swap the sides over we get:

$$r = \frac{100}{2\pi} = \frac{100}{2 \times 3 \cdot 14159} = \frac{100}{6 \cdot 28318} = 15 \cdot 9155$$

Now we can put this answer for r for into the area formula.

Area $= \pi r^2 = \pi \times 15 \cdot 9155^2 = 3 \cdot 14159 \times 253 \cdot 3 = 795 \cdot 77$

So the circle area of 795·77 m² is a lot bigger than the square which was only 625 m². In fact the biggest area you can mark out with a fence will always be a circle if you are on a flat surface. But if you just happen to be on a small green moon...

How many snaps does it take to break up a chocolate bar?

You start with a rectangular bar of chocolate and want to break it all into separate chunks. How many times do you have to snap it?

ONE WAY OF BREAKING UP A 3×2 CHOCOLATE BAR

Here we've got a little bar with just six chunks and it's taken us five snaps to break it up. But could you break it up with four snaps or fewer?

How many snaps will you need to break up a bigger bar?

These two bars both have 12 chunks. Which will break with fewer snaps, or will they both need the same number?

The answer is that it doesn't matter how you break a chocolate bar up, the number of snaps needed will always be one less than the number of chunks! Both these bars will need 11 snaps.

Once you know the answer, the reason for it becomes obvious. Every time you snap a piece off, the total number of separate pieces of chocolate increases by one. With the 12-chunk bar of chocolate, you're starting with one big piece. You finish with 12 small pieces, so the number of extra pieces you need to make is $12 - 1 = 11$.

How many chops do you need to divide a chocolate cube?

You have a nice big cube of chocolate and want to cut it into 27 smaller cubes. One way to do it is to divide it into three in each direction. If you don't move any of the pieces around until you've finished, then you'll need to make six straight cuts.

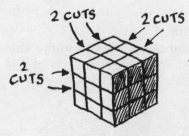

2 CUTS   2 CUTS

2 CUTS →

TOTAL PIECES
$= 3 \times 3 \times 3 = 27$

But supposing you're allowed to move the pieces around in between each cut? For example you start by chopping an end off, then put it underneath the bigger section so that the second cut goes through both pieces.

CUT OFF BIT LAID UNDERNEATH

SECOND CUT GOES DOWN THIS LINE

Can you divide the chocolate into 27 cubes with fewer than six cuts?

Answer: No! You will always need six cuts.

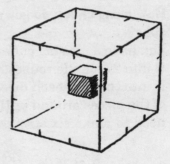

The reason is that one of the 27 cubes comes from the very centre of the block, so it doesn't have any flat sides of its own to start with. As this little cube needs six sides, it will take six separate cuts to make them.

How many different nets of a cube are there?

A **net of a cube** is a pattern made of six squares which can be folded to make a cube. The cross shape is probably the most obvious one but there are 11 cube nets in total! (That doesn't count rotations or reflections.)

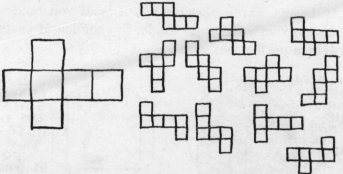

Hang on! What's happened here? There are *twelve* nets – and one of them smells rather suspiciously like old rotten fish. Oh no ... not another note!

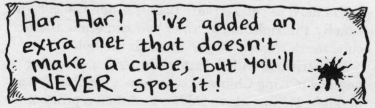

Har Har! I've added an extra net that doesn't make a cube, but you'll NEVER spot it!

Can you work out which of the 12 nets will *not* make a cube? (You can find out the answer on page 93.)

What is the biggest hole you can cut in a cube?

This might seem like a silly question but it has a really strange answer, and it's all thanks to this bloke:

IF YOU HAVE TWO CUBES THE SAME SIZE, YOU CAN CUT A HOLE IN ONE OF THEM BIG ENOUGH FOR THE OTHER TO PASS THROUGH.

Prince Rupert 1619–1682

It doesn't sound possible but it is. If you hold a cube at exactly the right angle, the shadow it casts will be a perfect hexagon.

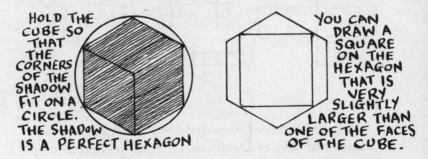

HOLD THE CUBE SO THAT THE CORNERS OF THE SHADOW FIT ON A CIRCLE. THE SHADOW IS A PERFECT HEXAGON

YOU CAN DRAW A SQUARE ON THE HEXAGON THAT IS VERY SLIGHTLY LARGER THAN ONE OF THE FACES OF THE CUBE.

You need to cut a square hole through the cube at exactly the right angle, then you can slide another cube *that's slightly bigger* through the hole!

This trick is called Prince Rupert's cube after a nephew of King Charles I who won a bet that it was possible. He was also a soldier and then a pirate and he invented all sorts of things including a type of gunpowder. Be honest, you didn't expect that lot from a maths genius, did you?

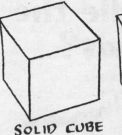
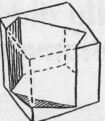

SOLID CUBE   CUBE WITH A HOLE IN IT
BIG ENOUGH FOR A SLIGHTLY
BIGGER CUBE TO PASS THROUGH

How big would a 1-tonne dice be if it was made of solid gold?

A cube of gold weighing 1 tonne would only measure about 37 cm along each edge.

How many ways can you mix up a Rubik's cube?

43,252,003,274,489,856,000.

If a computer could count 1,000 patterns per second, it would take about 1·4 million years to count them all. Experts have proved that *any* jumbled up Rubik's cube can be solved in 26 moves or less. Some people even suspect it might be possible with just 17 moves.

Did Dolly diddle the dodgy diamonds?

It's Tuesday lunchtime and the door of Carratt's Jewel Joint opens. In wafts a thick cloud of perfume all wrapped around a lady in a pink coat and hat.

"Miss Snowlips!" The eager man behind the counter adjusts his spotty bow tie and then hurries out to meet her. "This is a delight!"

"Hi, Sparkly," says Dolly Snowlips. "I've taken a fancy to that big blue diamond ring in the window. How much?"

"To you, $100," says Sparkly Carratt.

"I'll take it!" says Dolly handing over the money. That was Tuesday lunchtime and everybody finished up happy. Now it's Wednesday morning and once again Dolly is back in the store. "You know, Sparkly," she says, "what's the point in just looking good when you can look *even* better?"

"I do so agree," says Sparkly with a glint in his eye. "Is there something else that caught your fancy?"

"There sure is," says Dolly. "The big white diamond necklace. How much is that?"

"That one is $200."

"Oh," says Dolly. "Well I can't afford the ring and the necklace, so can I give you the ring back? It's worth $100."

"Certainly, Miss Snowlips," says Sparkly, taking the ring and passing over the necklace.

"I'm glad that's settled then, Sparkly," says Dolly opening the door.

"Just a minute, Miss Snowlips," says Sparkly worriedly. "You only gave me the ring, and we agreed that was worth $100. The necklace is $200, so what about the other $100?"

"Are you forgetting?" asks Dolly. "I gave you $100 yesterday."

"But that was for the ring!"

"I know, but I gave you the ring back," says Dolly. "Well I'll be seeing ya. Goodbye!"

And as Dolly's heels go clickety-clack away down the street, Sparkly Carratt is left wondering if he's just been cheated out of $100.

Answer:
Yes of course Sparkly was cheated! We need to add up everything that Dolly and Sparkly gave to each other.

Dolly gave Sparkly $100 and the ring (worth $100). Total = $200

Sparkly gave Dolly the ring ($100) and the necklace ($200). Total = $300.

85

Why can't you get a giant people-eating spider?

Place: Giant Spider Island
Date: 31 August 1929
Time: 10:45 am

The seven men were all huddled nervously in the back of the cave. Blade nudged Half-Smile who was still clutching the map. "Are you sure you read it right?" he asked.

"Sure I'm sure," nodded Half-Smile glumly. "This place is called Giant Spider Island."

"Eeek!" said the men.

"Oh, come on guys," said Blade trying to look brave. "What's so bad about a giant spider?"

"Are you kidding?" asked Chainsaw. "They've got eight hairy legs."

"So? We've got fourteen hairy legs," said Blade. "It's the spider that should be scared of us."

"But spiders are mean," said Chainsaw. "They get you all stuck up in their spiderwebs so you can't move then they slowly eat you alive until you're dead."

"Urghhhh!" Outside the sun was shining but the men all shuddered in cold fear.

"Let's be reasonable, guys," said Blade. "How big do we think this spider could be?"

"I read about a bird-eating spider once," said One-Finger Jimmy. "And that's for real."

"If you can have a bird-eating spider, why not a dog-eating spider?" asked Chainsaw.

"Or a horse-eating spider?" asked Weasel.

"Or a huge spider that spins a web big enough to drag ships full of screaming sailors down to their doom?" said Porky.

"Can they really make spiders that big?" said Blade.

Amazingly enough, we can answer Blade's question with some Murderous Maths. If we start with a normal spider and make it bigger, the body will get heavier, but can we make the legs strong enough to take the extra weight?

Let's pop down to the MM research lab where we've got some normal-sized spiders that are specially designed to make sums simple. (The Murderous Maths Organization would like to assure you that no spiders are hurt during the course of these sums.*)

Our special spiders are about the size of a big pea. They have a cube shaped body and their legs are like long square tubes. Suppose the body measures 10 mm × 10 mm × 10 mm. The volume will be 1,000 cubic millimetres which we can write as 1,000 mm³.

Don't worry too much about what a cubic millimetre is right now. All that's important is that the weight depends on the volume.

*That's because we do the sums first and when we've finished we squish them afterwards. We are murderous, after all.

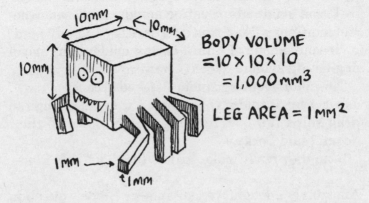

BODY VOLUME
$= 10 \times 10 \times 10$
$= 1,000 \text{ mm}^3$

LEG AREA $= 1 \text{ mm}^2$

The strength of a spider-leg depends on its cross-sectional area. Our special spider-legs measure 1 mm × 1 mm which makes an area of 1 square millimetre or 1 mm². You don't need to worry about square millimetres either. All that matters is that if each of the eight legs has an area of 1 mm², that's enough to hold up a body of 1,000 mm³.

If we made the spider bigger so that the volume was 2,000 mm³ then the legs would each need an area of 2 mm². A volume of 3,000 mm³ would need a leg area of 3 mm² and so on. For any size of spider, you divide the body volume by 1,000 to get the leg area it needs.

Now suppose we made our spider five times bigger in each direction so that it was about the size of a tangerine. The body volume would be 50 mm × 50 mm × 50 mm = 125,000 mm³. This volume needs a leg area of 125 mm².

BUT … the area of the legs for this spider would be

5 mm × 5 mm = 25 mm². The legs would be far too thin to hold the body up! In fact now that the body is five times longer in each direction, the legs need to be a lot more than five times thicker. They actually need to measure about 11 mm × 11 mm which would give an area of 121 mm² which is only just about enough.

(This is why in real life, little spiders can have very thin legs but bigger spiders have much fatter-looking legs.)

BIGGER SPIDERS NEED MUCH FATTER LOOKING LEGS...

OI! FAT LEGS!

Now suppose we made our spider body 100 times bigger in each direction so that it was about as big as an armchair. This would make our spider into a reasonable size to eat people, but before anybody panics, let's do the sums.

Each side of the body would measure 1,000 mm. The volume would be 1,000 mm × 1,000 mm × 1,000 mm = 1,000,000,000 mm³. This needs a leg area of 1,000,000 mm², so each leg would need to measure 1,000 mm × 1,000 mm. This means that one leg would completely fill the whole of one of the

89

square sides of the spider. The spider only has six sides, so two of the eight legs wouldn't even be able to fit on.

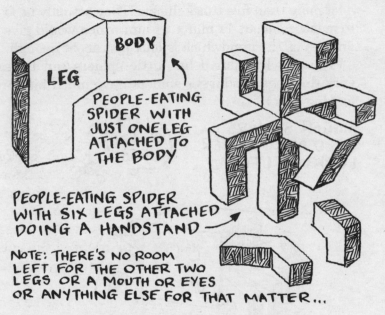

BODY

LEG

PEOPLE-EATING SPIDER WITH JUST ONE LEG ATTACHED TO THE BODY

PEOPLE-EATING SPIDER WITH SIX LEGS ATTACHED DOING A HANDSTAND —

NOTE: THERE'S NO ROOM LEFT FOR THE OTHER TWO LEGS OR A MOUTH OR EYES OR ANYTHING ELSE FOR THAT MATTER...

Therefore you can't possibly have a massive great big people-eating spider, so next time you see one, just get your calculator out and prove to it that it can't exist.

Meanwhile Weasel had given the gang an idea. They had raided the laundry boat and now were back inside the cave busy patching together all the sheets, towels, vests and socks into one big cloth shape.

"Why has this shape got to have two long sides and two short sides?" asked Blade.

"We're making a giant kite!" said the small man.

"If we fly it, people will see it from miles away. Somebody's bound to come and investigate."

"I guess we have to believe him," said Chainsaw. "We need rescuing and fast. I don't want to be around if there is a giant spider living here."

"Hey guys!" said Jimmy looking out of the cave. "There's a boat on the horizon! We got to get this thing in the air before it sails off."

"Any sign of the spider?" asked Blade.

"Not so far," said Jimmy. "So come on, let's move it!"

They all heaved the mass of cloth outside and then spread it out on the sand. Chainsaw and Porky dragged over two long bamboo poles and fitted them across the middle. Half-Smile had fetched a rope from the boat to use as the kite string. When it was all put together, Blade and Weasel stood the huge cloth shape upright. The others all grabbed the end of the rope and got ready to run down the beach and pull the kite up into the air.

Weasel was looking a bit worried. "The shape doesn't look right to me," he said.

"It better be right for your sake," said Blade. "You're the one who told us that a kite has to have two short sides and two long sides."

"Sure, that's what I said but..."

"And we've got two short sides and two long sides, so what's the problem?"

"It still don't look right," said Weasel.

"Who cares how it looks?" said Blade. "We just want it in the air before that boat goes. Ready, you guys? CHARGE!"

The five other men all dashed down the beach and the rope yanked the big cloth shape up into the air.

"There she goes!" said Blade.

"And round and round she goes," said Weasel. "And down she comes."

Blade and Weasel dived out of the way as the kite came crashing down between them.

"Told you it didn't look right," said Weasel. "That shape will never fly!"

To be continued…

What's that nasty thing in the basement?

If you don't believe our spider calculations, you're welcome to have a look in our research lab. Don't worry, it's nice and clean and perfectly safe. You go down the stairs, and hello ... what's this? Someone's dropped some scraps of paper on the floor.

Gosh! These are more of those extra questions that have been turning up in the book. It's time to find out who's responsible, so push open the door, and step inside and ... eek! Someone has just turned all the lights off. You grope your way forwards and stumble into a giant sticky cobweb. Yuk! Gazing out of tho shadows at you is something with nasty beady eyes and hairy legs that eats dead flies. Is it a giant spider after all? No, it's worse. It's your arch enemy Professor Fiendish with one of his diabolical challenges.

The professor clicks on a light. You see a row of dusty shelves stacked with boxes of all different sizes with air holes in the sides.

"This is my own private spider collection," he says. "There's the yellow-toed butter spider, and the Japanese bouncing spider and the very rare nine-legged chiming spider. In fact there are 120 spiders in here all of different weights between 1 kg and 120 kg. If you want to get out of here, you have to weigh them all!"

He shows you a set of balance scales and a box of 120 different weights, one for each spider.

"That's easy enough," you say.

"You haven't heard the evil bit," he cackles a bit evilly. "Here it comes!"

What is the smallest number of weights you need for a set of balance scales?

"I'll give you a clue," he says smugly. "To measure up to 120 kg you just need seven different weights, so decide which ones you need because I'm taking the rest away!"

How diabolical. If you don't want to be stuck forever in the spider den, which seven weights should you use?

The secret is that each weight you pick should be twice as heavy as the last one. If you only had four weights, they should be 1, 2, 4 and 8 kg and these would let you weigh anything up to 15 kg. Here's how:

THE WEIGHT YOU WANT TO WEIGH

	1	2	3	4	5	6	7	8	9	10	11	12	13	14	15
1	•		•		•		•		•		•		•		•
2		•	•			•	•			•	•			•	•
4				•	•	•	•					•	•	•	•
8								•	•	•	•	•	•	•	•

BLOBS SHOW WHICH WEIGHTS TO USE

HOW TO WEIGH AN 11KG SPIDER USING 8KG+2KG + 1KG WEIGHTS ——>

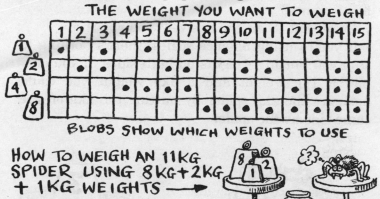

If you can have seven weights, the complete set should be 1, 2, 4, 8, 16, 32 and 64. (We can write these numbers out as 1, 2, 2^2, 2^3, 2^4, 2^5, 2^6.) If you put them all together they weigh 127 kg. You can weigh any smaller amount by missing a few weights out. For example you can weigh 107 kg with $1 + 2 + 8 + 32 + 64$ or you can weigh 94 kg with $2 + 4 + 8 + 16 + 64$.

"Oh really, my dear chap!" you tell the professor. "This is so simple it's hardly worth my time."

"Bah!" curses the professor. "In that case I'll make it harder." He grabs all the even-numbered weights and throws them down a drain. Your 2, 4, 8, 16, 32, and 64 have all gone! "Now see if you can weigh my spiders with seven other weights!"

You ponder the weights and the balance scales for a few seconds.

"Actually I only need five different weights," you tell him.

"Eh? Gasp? What?" says the professor. "But how can you measure anything up to 120kg with just five weights?"

"Now that IS an evil answer," you chuckle.

If you're using balance scales, there's nothing to stop you putting weights on both sides. If you only had a 1kg weight and a 3kg weight you could measure the 2kg spider by putting the 1kg on the same side as the spider.

You can tell the professor that the only weights you need are 1, 3, 9, 27 and 81. (Each weight is three times as big as the last one, so we could write them out as 1, 3, 3^2, 3^3, 3^4.)

Although it seems hard to believe, these five weights will let you measure any spider you like up to a maximum of 121 kg. Here's how you'd weigh the 97 kg spider.

"Honestly, Professor," you say as you pull yourself from the web, "you must try to make your questions a bit harder."

"Harder? HARDER?" he screams. "If you want harder questions, try this lot!"

He reaches into his pocket and pulls out a fistful of papers covered in extra mystery questions.

"Ha!" you say mockingly. "Is that the best you can do? We've already answered lots of these extra questions of yours. Give up now!"

"Me? Give up? NEVER!" he curses. "There's always another question, each one harder than the last."

"Sorry, can't be bothered."

"I think you'll be bothered with this next one." The professor pulls out a radio control panel and pushes some buttons. "Because I'm in control of your BATHROOM and I've just turned on both your bath taps!"

"But the plug isn't in," you answer.

"Har har!" he cackles. "I know! That's because it's all part of my next diabolical question..."

Will the bath overflow with both taps on but the plug left out?

Luckily you just happen to be carrying the instruction manual for your bath which includes all the technical specifications. To answer the professor's question, you need to work out what happens in one minute.

THE **HOT TAP** CAN FILL THE BATH IN 10 MINUTES

THE **COLD TAP** CAN FILL THE BATH IN 8 MINUTES

THE **PLUG HOLE** CAN EMPTY THE FULL BATH IN 5 MINUTES

If the hot tap takes 10 minutes to fill the bath, in one minute it can fill $1 \div 10 = 0 \cdot 1$ of the bath.

The cold tap takes 8 minutes to fill the bath, so in one minute it can fill $1 \div 8 = 0 \cdot 125$ of the bath.

If both taps are running then in one minute they will fill $0 \cdot 1 + 0 \cdot 125 = 0 \cdot 225$ of the bath.

Now suppose a full bath can empty in 5 minutes. After 1 minute the bath can lose $1 \div 5 = 0 \cdot 2$ of the water.

The water coming into the bath is $0 \cdot 225$ every minute, and the water going out is $0 \cdot 2$. Therefore if you have both taps on and the plug out, there's more water coming into the bath than there is leaving, your bath WILL overflow!

"Hadn't you better dash?" sneers the professor. "Any second now tons of water will be pouring over the top and running out into the landing."

"Tum tee tum," you say as you casually stroll towards the door. "Plenty of time!"

"How do you know?" he snaps.

"Oh really Professor, that's just too easy."

The exact fraction of the bath that fills every minute is $0.225 - 0.2 = 0.025$. This is the same as a fraction of $\frac{1}{40}$. So if one fortieth of the bath is filling every minute, to fill the complete bath will take 40 minutes.

You've got plenty of time to stroll along and turn the taps off, and you'd better pick up a clean towel and some soap along the way. After you've been stuck in the professor's giant cobweb you'll need a good bath!

How many people in the world share your birthday?

The population of the world is about 6,800,000,000 which is nearly seven billion. There are $365\frac{1}{4}$ days in the year, so the number of people who have their birthday on each day is $6{,}800{,}000{,}000 \div 365\frac{1}{4}$. This means that most of us share our birthday with about 18,617,000 people.

If you were born on 29th February, then you only have one proper birthday in every four years which is 1,461 days. You only have to share your birthday with $6{,}800{,}000{,}000 \div 1461 = 4{,}654{,}000$ people.

What are the chances of sharing your birthday with your mum...

There are 365 days in the calendar year. (We won't count leap years as they hardly make any difference for these sums.) Your chance of being born while your mum is blowing the candles out and opening her presents is $\frac{1}{365} = 0{\cdot}0027$ or $0{\cdot}27\%$.

...AND your granny?

First your mum has to be born on granny's birthday, so her chance of that is $\frac{1}{365}$ and then you have to be born on that date too. To combine these chances you multiply them together and get $\frac{1}{365} \times \frac{1}{365} = \frac{1}{133225}$ which comes to $0{\cdot}0000075$ or $0{\cdot}00075\%$.

It might sound very unlikely, but the fraction $\frac{1}{133225}$ tells you that out of every 133,225 people, the chances are that one person will share a birthday with mum and granny. The population of the world is 6,800,000,000 so if we divide this by 133,225 we find that there are about 51,000 mum/granny birthday sharers on the planet.

What are the chances that 365 strangers all have different birthdays?

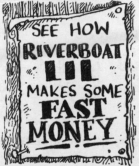

It's a big question with a big answer, so let's mosey on down to the Last Chance Saloon. It's just opened for the evening so we'll see how the birthday sums work out as the people arrive. To start with, Cliff the bartender is on his own, so there's no one he can share his birthday with yet. This means that his chance of not sharing = 1 or 100%.

CLIFF'S CHANCES OF NOT SHARING HIS BIRTHDAY = 1 OR 100%

Riverboat Lil arrives, so there is a very small chance that she will share Cliff's birthday. There are 365 days in the year (not counting leap years). 364 of these days will not be Cliff's birthday so her chance of not sharing with Cliff is $\frac{364}{365}$ = 0·997 or 99·7%

TWO PEOPLE'S CHANCES OF NOT SHARING A BIRTHDAY $= \frac{364}{365} = 0.997$ OR 99.7%

If Lil and Cliff do have different birthdays, then what happens when Duke turns up? There are only 363 days left in the year so his chance of not sharing with the others is $\frac{363}{365}$. To find the chances that none of the three people share, we need to combine Duke's chance with Lil's chance and we do it by multiplying them together.

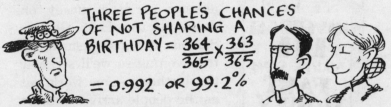

THREE PEOPLE'S CHANCES OF NOT SHARING A BIRTHDAY $= \frac{364}{365} \times \frac{363}{365}$
$= 0.992$ OR 99.2%

You'll see the chance of three people not sharing is smaller than two people, and the chance gets smaller and smaller as more people come into the saloon. Something slightly strange happens when the 23rd person arrives. The sum is:

$$\frac{364}{365} \times \frac{363}{365} \times \frac{362}{365} \times \dots \text{ all the way down to } \dots \times \frac{344}{365} \times \frac{343}{365}$$

There are 22 fractions to multiply, but don't worry. We've done it for you and the answer is 0·4927 or 49·27%. This tells us that if you have 23 people in a room the chance of them all having different birthdays is less than 50%. Therefore it is slightly more likely that at least two of them WILL share a birthday!

By the time 30 people have arrived at the saloon, Lil is ready to make some easy money!

You have to be careful with Riverboat Lil. She knows every strange trick that numbers can play. Even though there are 365 days in the year, if there are just 30 people in a room, there is a 70% chance that at least two will share a birthday! She takes this bet every night, and expects to win at least two times out of three. This trick is quite well known, but it does involve asking 30 people what their birthdays are. This can take a few minutes, but when there are about 70 people in the room Lil has a quicker trick. She just needs to find a group of six people, and they each have to shout their birthday out.

The exact sums for this are very murderous, but we can see roughly how it works. If there are 70 people in the room, most of them will have different birthdays. Therefore out of the 365 days in the year, roughly 300 will not be anybody else's birthday.

When the first of the six people shouts a birthday out, the chance of it not being shared is about $\frac{300}{365}$ which is about $\frac{5}{6}$. When the second person shouts out his birthday, there is also a chance of $\frac{5}{6}$ that he doesn't share it. To get the chances that neither of them share a birthday we multiply to get $\frac{5}{6} \times \frac{5}{6} = \frac{25}{36}$ = 69%. When all six people have shouted their birthdays, the chances of all of them not sharing are $\frac{5}{6} \times \frac{5}{6} \times \frac{5}{6} \times \frac{5}{6} \times \frac{5}{6} \times \frac{5}{6} = \frac{15625}{46656}$ or about 33%. Therefore there is roughly a 67% chance that at least one of the six people will share a birthday with somebody else!

Meanwhile the saloon is filling nicely and the 365th person has just arrived wearing snakeskin boots and a coal black hat.

MERCY ME! IT'S BRETT SHUFFLER!

I SEE LIL'S BEEN WINNING MONEY AGAIN.

IT COMES FROM FOLK SHARING THEIR BIRTHDAYS, BRETT.

WELL, ONE DAY THERE'S GONNA BE 365 PEOPLE AND NONE OF 'EM WILL SHARE AND THEN YOU'LL LOSE!

WANNA BET?

So what are the chances that 365 strangers all have a different birthday? Here's the sum:

$$\frac{364}{365} \times \frac{363}{365} \times \ldots \text{ all the way down to } \ldots \times \frac{2}{365} \times \frac{1}{365}$$

and the answer is:

= 0.0000000000 0000000000 0000000000 0000000000
0000000000 0000000000 0000000000 0000000000
0000000000 0000000000 0000000000 0000000000
0000000000 0000000000 0000000000 0000145496%

We've tried to keep the sums simple by ignoring leap years, but we are well aware that somewhere on the Earth right now there will be somebody reading this book who is demanding to know "What is the chance of 366 people in a room all with different birthdays?" If that person is YOU then go and look at *www.murderousmaths.co.uk*. And be warned – the numbers involved are not pretty.

The sums for people sharing birthdays are very similar to the sums for when you throw a few dice. It's no wonder that Riverboat Lil can also make money on dice, as Brett Shuffler is about to find out.

What's easier — throwing dice to all land with the same number or all land differently?

Brett is right. It is a lot easier to have NO matching numbers than it is to get all six dice landing the same.

Let's see how the sums work out by throwing two dice, one at a time. The first die can land on any number. There are six numbers on the die so the chance of the second die giving the same number is $\frac{1}{6}$ or about 17%. The chance of the second die being different is $\frac{5}{6}$ or 83%, so it's much more likely for the two dice to be different.

Here are how the sums work out for more dice. (For these sums, when you throw three or more dice, they either have to be ALL the same or ALL different. We ignore results such as 2, 4, 4 or 1, 3, 3, 3, 5.)

The chances of the dice landing...	
...all the same	**...all different**
$\frac{1}{6} = 17\%$	$\frac{5}{6} = 83\%$
$\frac{1}{6} \times \frac{1}{6} = 3\%$	$\frac{5}{6} \times \frac{4}{6} = \frac{20}{36} = 55\%$
$\frac{1}{6} \times \frac{1}{6} \times \frac{1}{6} = 0.46\%$	$\frac{5}{6} \times \frac{4}{6} \times \frac{3}{6} = \frac{60}{216} = 55\%$
$\frac{1}{6} \times \frac{1}{6} \times \frac{1}{6} \times \frac{1}{6}$ $= 0.077\%$	$\frac{5}{6} \times \frac{4}{6} \times \frac{3}{6} \times \frac{2}{6} = \frac{120}{1296}$ $= 9\%$
$\frac{1}{6} \times \frac{1}{6} \times \frac{1}{6} \times \frac{1}{6} \times \frac{1}{6}$ $= 0.012\%$	$\frac{5}{6} \times \frac{4}{6} \times \frac{3}{6} \times \frac{2}{6} \times \frac{1}{6}$ $= 1.5\%$

As you can see, when Brett throws six dice, his chance of getting all the dice different is only about 1·5%. Suppose he had 200 tries. He would only expect to win 200 × 1·5% = about 3 times, so Lil would only pay him 3 × $50 = $150. However his 200 tries would cost him $200. Lil would slowly end up taking all his money!

The interesting thing is that it doesn't matter how many dice are being thrown, it's always easier to get them all different rather than all the same. Or is it...?

What was Lil's sneaky secret?

Answer: They were playing with SEVEN six-sided dice. Although Lil's chances of throwing them all the same were only 1 in 46,656, Brett had NO chance of throwing them all different!

The shortest link

Meanwhile up on Lunagoll, the Ploogs have got bored and left. The Gollarks find the Ploogs have built a power system which has four different units laid out in a square pattern. Each side of the square measures 100 metres. The Ploogs have also left a roll of wire. To make the system work the four units all need connecting together, but there's a problem...

If the Gollarks connect the units along the diagonals of the square with the wires all joining up in the middle, will it use less wire? This leads to a good question...

How long is the diagonal of the square?

Each diagonal d is the long side of a right-angled triangle where the other sides are both 100 metres. Pythagoras' Theorem says that:

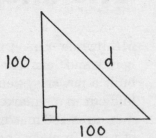

$d^2 = 100^2 + 100^2 = 10,000 + 10,000 = 20,000$

Therefore d = $\sqrt{20,000}$ = 141·42 metres.

The Gollarks need enough wire for two diagonals, so 2 × 141·42 = 282·84 metres. It is less than the 400 metres their first plan needed, but unfortunately they only have 280 metres so they still can't quite connect the four units.

Oh dear, they've given up. But why did the Ploogs leave 280 metres of wire? They are obviously more intelligent than the Gollarks, so did they have a better way to connect up their power system?

What is the shortest way to connect the corners of a square?

Whenever you're connecting three or more things together, it's called a network. To use the shortest amount of wire, you should make the wires meet at angles of 120°.

When the Ploogs connected up their four units, the wires would have looked like this. All the angles where the wires meet are 120°.

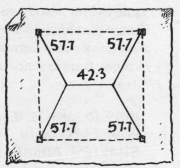

The lengths of each piece of wire are marked in, so how much wire is needed in total?

It's 4 × 57·7 + 42·3 = 273·1 metres.

So the 280 metres of wire would have been enough after all!

Is there a very strange way of proving this by using bubbles?

Yes. Isn't that great?

You get two sheets of glass. On one of them you fix four thin pegs sticking up to show where the corners of the square are, then you fix the other sheet of glass on top. You then slosh a lot of bubble mixture between the two sheets. Once the bubbles have settled down, the films of bubble will show the shortest way of linking the pegs up! This is because flat sheets of bubble film will always shrink to find the shortest route, and whenever three bits of flat bubble join together they make an angle of 120°.

This 120° rule doesn't just work with

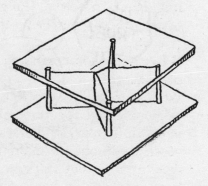

squares and power units, it applies to any network of things that need linking up. If you wanted to connect a set of six water fountains, the shortest arrangement of pipes you need should all meet at 120°.

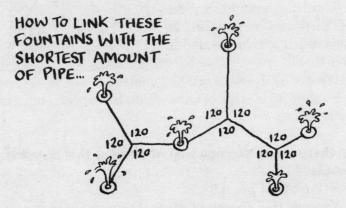

HOW TO LINK THESE FOUNTAINS WITH THE SHORTEST AMOUNT OF PIPE...

120 120 120 120 120 120 120 120 120 120 120

ALL ANGLES BETWEEN PIPES = 120 DEGREES

If you don't believe it, then ask an expert.

IT'S TRUE!

POP!

A lot of hot air

It's Veronica Gumfloss's birthday, and so Pongo has organized a special treat for her.

How many blows would it take to blow up a hot air balloon?

A balloon big enough to carry two people would need a volume of about 1,200 cubic metres. It's going to be more helpful to have the volume in litres so as there are 1,000 litres in a cubic metre, this gives us a volume of 1,200 × 1,000 = 1,200,000 litres.

We need to divide this volume by the amount of air Pongo can blow out in one go. Most people can blow out about 3 litres in one huge puff (although a big fit athlete might manage 6 litres or more.)

Therefore the total number of blows would be 1,200,000 ÷ 3 = 400,000 blows.

How long would it take?

One deep breath and blow out takes about 5 seconds, so the total time would be 400,000 × 5 = 2,000,000 seconds. That's more than three weeks without stopping!

Please note: the Murderous Maths Organization does not wish to offend readers of a sensitive disposition. Therefore we shall use a polite name when referring to the little bursts of hot gas produced by Pongo's peppered sprout soup.

How many pant rattlers does it take to fill a hot air balloon?

The average pant rattler has a volume of 0·05 litres. (Experts measure this by adding washing-up liquid to their bathwater and then calculating the volumes of any bubbles that are produced while they are lying back reading the newspaper.)

If the balloon volume = 1,200,000 litres then the number of pant rattlers required = 1,200,000 ÷ 0·05 = 24,000,000.

The answer is that it takes 24 million pant rattlers

to fill a smallish hot air balloon. Bigger hot air balloons can be· over 15,000,000 litres and these would require at least 300 million pant rattlers. This information is useful for making pleasant conversation if you're ever out with a group of posh friends and you see a beautiful big balloon rising majestically into the sky.

How do you make a perfect kite shape quickly?

Place: Giant Spider Island, Pacific Ocean
Date: 31 August 1929
Time: 11:10 a.m.

The boat on the horizon was still there, but it would be gone soon. On the beach the men stared in despair at their giant kite.

"Two sides are short and two sides are long," muttered Blade. "So why doesn't it fly?"

"Like I said, it's the wrong shape," said Weasel. "It needs a pointy bottom."

"We'll have to take it all apart and start again," said Porky.

"We don't have time!" said Blade. "We've only got time to make one cut and then stitch it up. How are we going to do this?"

The usual kite shape isn't the only one with "two short sides and two long sides". You can also have a parallelogram or a rectangle. Blade's shape was a rectangle, but luckily for him you only need one cut to change it into a kite shape.

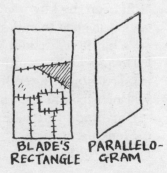

BLADE'S RECTANGLE   PARALLELO- GRAM

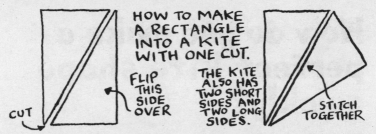

The two angles on the sides of a kite shape should be the same, and the kite usually looks better if these angles are both 90°. That's what you get when you cut a rectangle and flip one side over!

"At last, the kite's got a pointy bottom," said Blade. "Now let's get it up there!"

"I just remembered, it needs one more thing," said Weasel.

"WHAT?" they said, gathering around the small man.

"It needs a tail or a weight or something hanging off the pointy bottom to keep it nice and steady in the air."

The men all looked around. There were plenty of rocks and boulders but nothing they could easily tie onto the end of the kite.

"Well?" said Weasel. "Come on, Blade, you're supposed to be the brains. What are you going to use?"

"I just thought of the perfect thing," said Blade. "It'll keep the kite nice and steady, and anybody who sees it is sure to sail straight over here."

"What is it?" asked Weasel.

Despite the tough situation, a cunning smile crossed Blade Boccelli's lips. "Guess," he said.

"Don't look at me," said Weasel.

But Blade *was* looking at him. In fact they were *all* looking at him.

To be continued...

What is the biggest number?

You can think of the biggest number you like and then add one and make it even bigger, so there's no limit to the biggest number. It's generally called infinity. So let's ask our Pure Mathematicians what is the biggest number apart from infinity?

INFINITY MINUS ONE! HO HO!

Oh very funny, but as it's impossible to imagine what infinity looks like, there's no point in counting down from it. The only way we can imagine big numbers is to start with some numbers we can understand then work upwards. First let's see a few silly little numbers to get us in the mood.

1,000 One thousand would be about the number of letters on this page if we hadn't put a picture there.

10,000 When the French invented the metric system of measurements they decided that the distance from the North pole down to the Equator should be ten thousand kilometres.

100,000 One hundred thousand is roughly the number of hairs on your head.

1,000,000 One million is about the number of grains of sand in one seaside bucket-sized sandcastle.

1,000,000 GRAINS OF SAND

How long does it really take to count to one million?

If you could count one number every second, then it would take you about 11 and a half days. It's not that easy though! Even if you didn't have to sleep or eat or watch your favourite programme, the numbers themselves cause trouble. When you start counting "one ... two ... three..." just saying one number every second might seem very slow, but pretty soon you'll be up against numbers like 54,911 (fifty four thousand, nine hundred and eleven) or 200,222 (two hundred thousand two hundred and twenty two) or 756,834 (seven hundred and fifty six thousand eight hundred and thirty four). Try saying one of these numbers every second!

Is there an easy way to write down big numbers?

Once you start going above a million it gets a bit boring writing out loads of zeros. You can describe a million as "one with six zeros after it" and there's a neat way of writing this out: 10^6. This works because:

$$10^6 = 10 \times 10 \times 10 \times 10 \times 10 \times 10 = 1,000,000.$$

Scientists use this a lot to describe big numbers.

If they wanted to write down 2,000,000 they would put 2×10^6. If they wanted to be a bit more accurate and write down 2,340,000 they would put $2 \cdot 34 \times 10^6$. The most important bit of this number is the tiny little ^{6} because it immediately tells them the number is in the millions. The 2·34 is just telling them how many millions they've got.

If a scientist saw the number $5 \cdot 718 \times 10^4$, the first thing they check is the little ^{4}. This tells them they are dealing with a number in the 10,000s.

What does 2·378I E9 on my calculator screen mean?

The E9 means you multiply $2 \cdot 3781 \times 10^9$ which is the same as $2 \cdot 3781 \times 1,000,000,000$. So 2·378 E9 = 2,378,100,000

What are a billion, a trillion and a quadrillion like?

10^9 1,000,000,000 = **one billion**

Here's where the fun starts:

- A billion used to be a million million i.e. 1,000,000,000,000 or 10^{12}. However the USA always had a billion as one thousand million, and generally the rest of the world can't be bothered to argue. That's probably because people who have more than $1,000,000,000 like being called billionaires. It's catchier than just being called "thousand millionaires".
- One billion pennies laid in a line would reach from the North pole round to the South pole.
- One billion blades of grass would cover about 20 football pitches.
- *Useless fact:* One billion is the smallest number in

the English language to have the same number of
letters as there are digits in the number.
1 0 0 0 0 0 0 0 0 0
o n e b i l l i o n

10^{12} 1,000,000,000,000 = **one trillion**
- A trillion pennies would cover a flat area a lot
  bigger than Birmingham.
- A trillion drops of water would fill about 20
  Olympic-size swimming pools.
- A trillion seconds is about 31,688 years.
- A trillion minutes is nearly two million years.
- A trillion hours ago was about 114 million years
  ago. The dinosaurs were in full swing and ants
  were just starting to appear. Can you imagine the
  giant dinosaurs fighting some tiny ants? Guess
  who wins? You'll get the results in a minute...

10^{15} 1,000,000,000,000,000 = **one quadrillion**
- Somebody has calculated that there are one
  quadrillion ants in the world. And there are no
  dinosaurs. So the ants won.

What's after a quadrillion?
We're now getting to the point where numbers start
to have very fancy names and it's impossible to
imagine what they look like, but that doesn't stop
them getting bigger! Here are a just few of them for
you to admire.

10^{22} **Ten sextillion** (10^{21} = one sextillion. There's
no special word for 10^{22}, but $10 \times 10^{21} = 10^{22}$.) This is
supposed to be the number of grains of sand on all

the beaches and deserts on Earth. This is enough sand to give every ant 10 little sandcastles to live in.

7×10^{27} **Seven octillion** Atoms in an adult human cowboy person in a black hat. (Yes, that's a 7 with 27 zeros after it.)

2×10^{36} **Two undecillion** How many ways Binkie can play six four-note chords on a piano. (See page 12.)

8×10^{67} **Eighty unvigintillion.** (10^{66} = one unvigintillion. There's no special word for 10^{67}.) Number of ways you can put a pack of 52 cards in order. You work this out by mutliplying $52 \times 51 \times 50 \times \dots$ all the way down to $\dots \times 3 \times 2 \times 1$.

10^{79} This is what some people think is the number of atoms in the universe. (They haven't quite finished counting them yet.) It's got an especially good name too...

10^{10^2} or 10^{100} This is a GOOGOL which is a 1 with 100 zeros after it.

$10^{10^{10^2}}$ or 10^{GOOGOL} This is a GOOGOLPLEX which is a 1 with a googol zeros after it.

Now you've got warmed up, it's time to look at the *top four famous big numbers* starting with the smallest.

The biggest prime number (found so far)

A prime number will only divide by itself and 1. Although there is no "biggest" prime number, the problem is finding them. Even as you read this book, there are massive banks of computers chugging away trying to find bigger and bigger primes. We're not going to print the biggest prime number found so far for two reasons:

1 By the time you read this, they might have found a bigger one.

2 In August 2008, they found a prime number with 12,978,189 digits, so it would fill about 200 copies of this book. If you really want to see it, you can work it out for yourself. Here's the formula: $2^{43,112,609} - 1$.

WARNING! If you decide to do this on a calculator, the screen will need to be over 50 km long.

Archimedes' Sand Reckoner

Over 2,000 years ago the Greek genius Archimedes decided to work out how many grains of sand it would take to completely fill up the universe. At the time, the biggest number anyone was using was the *myriad* which was 10,000 (which is 10^4).

He decided to beef the myriad up by multiplying it by itself to get a *myriad myriads* which is 100,000,000 (or 10^8).

He then multiplied a *myriad myriads* by itself a *myriad myriad* times, and then multiplied the answer by itself another *myriad myriad* times. He ended up with a number that was a 1 followed by 80,000,000,000,000,000 zeros.

Skewes' Number

This beauty is also linked to prime numbers. Between 0 and 100 there are 25 prime numbers. Between 101 and 200 there are 21 primes. Between 201 and 300 there are 16 primes. Prime numbers seem to get rarer the higher you go, but back in 1933 Samuel Skewes showed that if you keep going high enough primes start to get more common again. So how high do you have to go?

I WORKED OUT THAT THE TURNING POINT HAD TO BE SOMEWHERE BEFORE $10^{10^{10^{34}}}$

This number is pretty big. To work it out you have to start with the littlest numbers up at the top.

$$10^{34} = 10,000,000,000,000,000,000,000,000,000,000,000$$

So far so good. Now we come down and bring in the next 10.

$10^{10^{34}}$ = 1 with 10^{34} zeros after it. (No, it's not a 1 with 34 zeros, we've already done that. It's a 1 followed by *ten million billion billion billion* zeros.) If we printed this number out in a line on this page, the page would need to be long enough to stretch across the universe about 10,000 times. (And it would be a bit boring to read.)

Although this number is massively bigger than Archimedes' Sand Reckoner, it's still a lot smaller than a googleplex. Don't be disappointed because we've still got to bring in the final 10.

This is a 1 and the number of zeros you have to write after it is that number you've just written out that went across the universe 10,000 times. Imagine dismantling the entire universe into single atoms. How many different ways do you think you could put them all back together again? It's that sort of number.

(Incidentally modern computers now think that the answer to Skewes' prime number problem is actually much smaller than this number. But we were looking for the *famous* answer, not necessarily the right answer.)

THAT'S A PRETTY BIG NUMBER, EH?

PAH! THAT'S PEANUTS! HERE'S THE NUMBER I INVENTED.

R.L. GRAHAM

What is the most famous number to hold the world record for being the biggest answer to a problem? And the answer is ... **Graham's Number.**

CALIFORNIA, 1977

RON! STOP JUGGLING! WE NEED YOUR HELP WITH RAMSEY'S THEOREM!

WOW!

LIKE CRAZY, MAN!

R L Graham was answering a problem with numbers so big that he had to use a special way of writing them. It's called **Knuth's up-arrow notation** after Donald Knuth who invented it. He started with 3^3 and wrote it as $3{\uparrow}3$ which is $3 \times 3 \times 3 = 27$. Then he did $3{\uparrow}{\uparrow}3$ which is $3^{3^3} = 3^{27} = 7{,}625{,}597{,}484{,}987$. As you can see, adding one or two more arrows does immensely silly things to the number. We're not even going to bother thinking about $3{\uparrow}{\uparrow}{\uparrow}{\uparrow}3$ as it's too big to fit on the planet. So imagine a number that goes $3{\uparrow}{\uparrow}{\uparrow}...{\uparrow}{\uparrow}{\uparrow}3$ and the number of arrows is $3{\uparrow}{\uparrow}{\uparrow}{\uparrow}3$.

And when you've got that number, you put that many arrows between two threes and work that out. And then do it again ... 63 times. Bingo! You've got Graham's number, which is supposed to be the biggest number that is an answer to a problem.

It's a fabulous answer, but just like Skewes before him, it seems that Mr Graham might have got a bit carried away.

So what was the problem?

Back in 1930, Frank Plumpton Ramsey proved that if you have enough things, you can always find a pattern. (He also proved that having a funny middle name doesn't stop your brother from being the Archbishop of Canterbury. It's true, his brother was the Archbishop!) For instance there are so many stars in the sky that somehow somewhere, eight of them must mark out the corners of a perfect cube.

There's a neat little game to show how it works. You need three different coloured pens. Black, red and green would be good.

- Draw a black circle and put some dots round the edge.
- Use the red and green pens to join every dot to every other dot with a straight line.
- You must *avoid making a complete triangle* in

either colour. (A complete triangle has to have dots at all three corners.)

- You can play with a friend if you each have a different pen and take turns to put the lines in. The first person to complete a triangle loses!

You'll find that you can avoid making a one-coloured triangle with three, four or five dots, but when you get to six dots or more it's impossible!

RAMSAY THEOREM GAME

HERE IS HOW THE
DOTS CAN BE JOINED
UP WITH DIFFERENT-COLOURED
LINES.

—— RED
~~~ GREEN

FOR CIRCLES WITH 3,4 OR 5 DOTS YOU CAN AVOID MAKING A TRIANGLE WITH ALL THREE SIDES THE SAME COLOUR.

(THIS LITTLE TRIANGLE WITH THREE RED SIDES DOESN'T COUNT BECAUSE THE CORNERS HAVE TO BE DOTS ON A CIRCLE.)

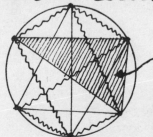

—— OH DEAR! THIS TRIANGLE HAS THREE RED SIDES!

WHEN YOU'RE JOINING UP SIX OR MORE DOTS, YOU CAN'T HELP IT!

If you allow yourself three different colours then you can avoid completing a triangle unless there are 17 or more dots (and there will be 136 lines to colour in!).

Otherwise you can stick to two colours but you have to avoid making a *four-sided* shape. If your circle has 18 or more dots it's impossible. Now suppose you have to avoid making a *five-sided* shape? Nobody knows the answer for the smallest number of dots to make it impossible but it's somewhere between 43 and 49. This seems a bit vague doesn't it?

As soon as you add in more colours and sides and a few extra dimensions, you start to get really vague and end up with an answer that could be anywhere between six and Graham's number. You can't get much vaguer than that!

The curry burger problem

Pongo has set his de-luxe burger bar up next to Kumar's restaurant "The Ravenous Rajah", and they are both having a special party offer on curry burgers. They each have a total of 30 curry burgers to sell and all the burgers are exactly the same.

- Pongo sells 3 burgers in a party bag, so if he has 30 burgers, that's enough for 10 bags. Each bag costs £12, so Pongo should hope to take 10 × £12 = £120.
- Kumar sells 2 burgers in a bag, so his 30 burgers will make 15 bags. Kumar's bags also cost £12, so he should take 15 × £12 = £180.
- The total money they should take between them is £120 + £180 = £300.

However Kumar is a bit worried that Pongo's burger bar is spoiling the look of his restaurant, so he politely offers Pongo a deal. He suggests that he'll take Pongo's burgers and sell them for him. As Pongo's burgers are 3 for £12 and Kumar's are 2 for £12, Kumar says the fairest thing to do is add these numbers, so that he'll sell 5 burgers for £24. Pongo agrees, so he hands over his burgers and goes away.

Now Kumar has 60 burgers to sell, and he's selling them in bags of 5. The total number of bags is 60 ÷ 5 = 12 bags. Each bag costs £24, so the total amount of money he should take is 12 × £24 = £288.

If Pongo and Kumar had sold their burgers separately, they would have taken £300. **Where has the missing £12 gone?**

Answer:

Pongo and Kumar should have worked out what they were each charging for one burger. Pongo was selling 3 for £12, his burgers cost £4 each. Kumar was selling 2 for £12 so his burgers were £6 each. The average price for each burger was (£4 + £6) ÷ 2 = £5. If you multiply this by the number of burgers for sale you get 60 × £5 = £300. This total is what Pongo and Kumar expected!

If Kumar wants to sell 5 burgers in each bag, he should charge 5 × the average price. That comes to 5 × £5 = £25. And sure enough, when he sells all 12 bags he'll get 12 × £25 = £300.

How high is a kite?

Place: Giant Spider Island, Pacific Ocean
Date: 31 August 1929
Time: 11:15 am

"Let me down!" yelped Weasel, whose feet were dangling just above the sand. Chainsaw Charlie and One-Finger Jimmy were holding up the kite, and the small man was hanging off it, tied on by his trouser braces.

"Stop moaning," said Blade. "You're the one who said the kite needed a weight tied to it. OK boys, take it away!"

The other men pulled on the end of the rope and sure enough, Weasel shot up into the air and then hovered high above the beach.

"Wow!" they all said. They tied the end of the rope to a big rock then stared out at the horizon. The boat was still there, but had the people on it noticed the kite? If so, they surely must have seen the small wriggling shape dangling off the bottom. They could probably hear it too.

"Let me down!" it screamed. "Let me DOWN!"

"Do you think Weasel's high enough?" asked Blade.

"That rope is 50 metres long," said Half-Smile. "But it doesn't go straight up, so he can't be that high."

"Then I guess there's no way of knowing exactly how high he is," said Blade. And at that exact moment Weasel's left shoe fell off and landed directly below him on the beach.

Actually Blade could have worked out exactly how high Weasel was by using Pythagoras' Theorem! He knows the rope is 50 metres, and he needs to measure the distance from where the rope meets the ground to where Weasel's shoe fell. Let's suppose it was 40 metres. This gives us enough measurements to complete a right-angled triangle.

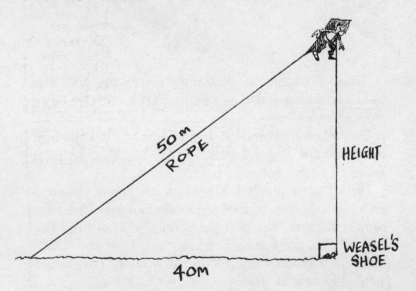

Thanks to Pythagoras we know that $height^2 + 40^2 = 50^2$.
Therefore $height^2 = 50^2 - 40^2 = 2500 - 1600 = 900$.
And finally $height = \sqrt{900} = 30$ metres.

But Pythagoras might have been a bit tricky for Blade, so here's another way he could have seen how high the kite was. Blade asks Jimmy to stand by Weasel's shoe. Blade holds a pencil out in front of his face so that the pencil seems to reach from Jimmy up to the kite. Blade then tips the pencil sideways and sees how far along the beach the end of the pencil comes. Jimmy walks along until he is in line with the pencil point. The distance Jimmy walks is the same as the height of the kite!

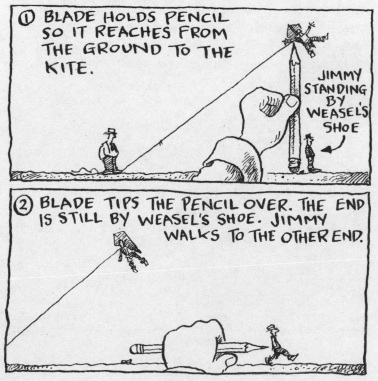

① BLADE HOLDS PENCIL SO IT REACHES FROM THE GROUND TO THE KITE.

JIMMY STANDING BY WEASEL'S SHOE

② BLADE TIPS THE PENCIL OVER. THE END IS STILL BY WEASEL'S SHOE. JIMMY WALKS TO THE OTHER END.

As long as Weasel was high enough to be noticed by the boat, then that was high enough. And it turned out that Weasel was high enough.

"The boat's turning!" shouted Weasel. "It's coming this way!"

The six men down on the beach gave a loud cheer.

"That's the good news," shouted Weasel.

"What's the bad news?" shouted Blade.

"It's the prison boat," said Weasel.

To be continued...

Can one giant sneeze blast the Earth out of orbit?

What a very good, sensible and highly intelligent question, especially if everybody in the world gets together and sneezes at once!

Dear Murderous Maths,
I wish to complain about the sneezing chapter. Sneeze germs can be very nasty and fly out at 100 m.p.h. Therefore you should always hold a tissue up to your nose and then throw it away.
Yours sincerely, Bo Ginnose.
P.S. You throw the tissue away. Not your nose.

Yes, yes, we know about nasty sneeze germs. But seeing as this book has already had giant spiders, aliens on random spinning moons, somebody dangling off a kite and Pongo McWhiffy's peppered sprout soup, we trust that our readers can work out what's sensible and what's not for themselves.

Dear Murderous Maths,
Very well. Just as long as you don't have lots of people sneezing into the same paper bag.
Yours sincerely, Bo Ginnose.

Ooh, now *there's* a thought...

So back to the question. To see how to work it out, imagine you have two ice skaters who are the same size. If they push each other away, they will move the same distance in opposite directions. But if one skater is three times bigger than the other, it will take three times as much force to move him, so he will only move $\frac{1}{3}$ of the distance. The fraction of $\frac{1}{3}$ comes from dividing the weight of the small skater by the weight of the big skater.

Instead of a big ice skater, we've got the Earth. Instead of a little ice skater we have a massive cloud of everybody's sneezy stuff moving in the opposite direction. The first thing we need to estimate is how far the sneezy stuff shoots out of your nose, so we'll say that most of it goes about one metre. For some people it will be less, but if sneezing ever becomes an Olympic sport you can be sure that other people will spend years training to get it to the far end of the long jump pit.

Next we need to see how much the sneezy stuff weighs, so let's pop down to Fogsworth Manor where Croak the butler has kindly agreed to help. Everyone has sat down to dinner, but none of them suspect that Croak is about to have a little "accident" with the pepper.

Never mind. Let's assume the average sneeze weighs about 10 grams which is 0·01 kg. As there are about 6,800,000,000 people on Earth, in total they'll fire off 6,800,000,000 × 0·01 kg = 68,000,000 kg of sneezy stuff. (That's the same as 68,000 tonnes which is enough to fill 2,000 lorries. How lovely.)

The weight of the Earth is about 6,000,000,000,000, 000,000,000,000 kg so if the sneezy stuff moves 1 metre then the Earth will move:

$$\frac{68,000,000}{6,000,000,000,000,000,000,000,000} \times 1 \text{ metres} =$$
$$0·00000000000000001133 \text{ metres}$$

This is about 1×10^{-17} metres or 10 *attometres*. This is about one fiftieth of a millionth of the width of a single atom. (See page 58.) So the answer is no, the Earth will not be blasted out of orbit.

This answer seems a bit disappointing when there's 68,000 tonnes of sneezy stuff being blasted away. Maybe we'd better test it. OK everybody, get your pepper ready and look upwards ... hang on! What's this? It seems that the Gollarks have got fed up of taking over moons and have decided to try and take over Earth instead. Luckily we're ready for them.

THE EARTHLINGS HAVE ALL GATHERED IN ONE PLACE !

The mysterious handcuffs

We've had tons of numbers and sums in the book, so just for a change we'll look at a completely different sort of maths called **topology**. All that matters are holes and how they are linked together, so to demonstrate what can happen we're going to use some special handcuffs. Be warned – what you're about to see is very peculiar!

How can you link the handcuffs without breaking them?
You can try this yourself by making some handcuffs out of Blu-tak. You start with the two loops that are separated and you have to finish with the loops linked together.

It looks impossible to do without breaking one loop open and closing it again, but look at the diagrams!

You won't believe it until you've tried it, and even then you probably still won't believe it.

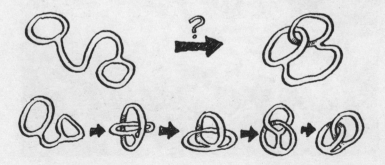

How can the handcuffs pass through a solid mug handle?

Here's where it gets even stranger. It's all very well fiddling about with a bit of Blu-tak on its own, but suppose we fix both loops of our handcuffs to something solid like a mug handle? Can you release one of the loops without breaking it and putting it back together?

It seems impossible doesn't it? But sometimes in the Murderous Maths Organization, the impossible is what we do best...

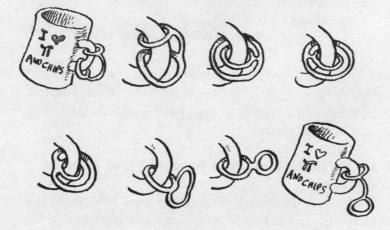

Some unexpectedly evil football sums

You might wonder why football gets into a book of awkward maths questions, because most things in football are very simple. If the score is 3–1 then one team has scored two goals more than the other one. That's simple isn't it? If a top footballer has £30 million and buys his girlfriend a car that costs £85,352.17 how much money has he got left? Let's ask him...

Yes, most things in football are very simple, but Murderous Maths fans needn't be disappointed. Football does have a few easy-looking questions with evil answers!

Where is the best place to score a goal from the touchline?
If you put the ball too near the goal line, then the goal will look very narrow. If you put the ball too far

away, then the goal will look tiny. What you want is for the goal to look as wide as possible.

If you draw lines to the goalposts, the angle between them shows how wide the goal looks. You need to kick from where the angle is widest.

Draw a circle that goes through the two goalposts and just touches the touchline. The point where it touches gives the biggest angle, so it's the best place to kick from!

(If you want to work out exactly where to stand it's a very difficult formula, but unless your goal is almost as wide as the pitch there's a simple answer. Say your pitch is W metres wide, you should stand about $\frac{W}{2}$ from the goal line.)

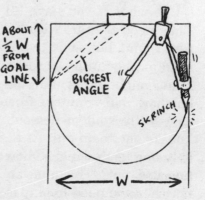

How many matches does a knockout competition need?

If you have a set of teams playing, the matches are usually drawn up like this.

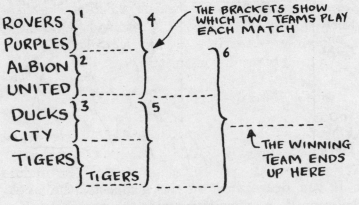

THE BRACKETS SHOW WHICH TWO TEAMS PLAY EACH MATCH

THE WINNING TEAM ENDS UP HERE

TIGERS HAD NO ONE TO PLAY IN THE FIRST ROUND

You'll see that these seven teams need to play a total of six matches before one of them wins. Tigers are lucky because there aren't quite enough teams to all play in the first round, so they skip a match.

But what if you have 29 teams? Or 317 teams? They need to start with a lot more matches in the first round, but some teams will be lucky and won't need to play until the second round.

You might think it would be murderous working out how many matches need to be played, but it's easy with a bit of devious thinking! Every match knocks one team out. At the end of the competition only one team wins, so how many teams have been knocked out? The answer is that the number of matches you need to play is always *one less than the total number of teams!*

How long does a goalkeeper have to save a penalty?

On a standard pitch, the penalty spot is 11 metres from where the goalkeeper is standing in the goal. The kicker can probably whack the ball at a speed of about 30 metres per second. (This is nearly 70 miles per hour.)

We need to use the equation:

time = distance ÷ speed (or $t = d/s$)

Therefore the time between the ball being kicked and reaching the goal is 11 ÷ 30 = 0·367 seconds.

Suppose the goalie was standing in the middle and didn't move until the ball was kicked. Even if he knew immediately that the the ball was going to shoot into the bottom corner of the goal, could he get to it? It takes about 0·5 of a second for a normal person to drop to the ground (whether you dive to the side or not), so the answer is no!

If you hit the goalpost, what are the chances of the ball going in the goal?

This is an incredibly awkward question, so before we start we have to assume that the ball is moving at 90° to the touchline and that the goalpost is square. We also have to assume that the goalie hasn't stuck his chewing gum on the bit that the ball is about to hit otherwise the ball just hits the post and stays there.

A standard football has a radius of about 11 cm and the maximum allowed width of a square goalpost is about 12 cm.

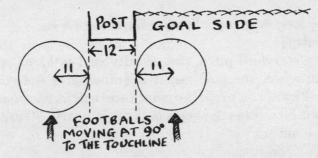

FOOTBALLS MOVING AT 90° TO THE TOUCHLINE

The two footballs in the diagram are just about to skim each side of the post. If the football is going to hit the post, the centre point of the ball can be anywhere between the centres of the two marked footballs. You can see that the total width of this target area is 11 + 12 + 11 = 34 cm.

If the ball hits the right-hand side of the post at an angle of 45°, it will shoot straight across to the side.

If it hits the post any further to the right, it will bounce on into the goal. Therefore we need to know how far across the centre of the ball needs to be for the ball to hit at 45°. Amazingly enough we need Pythagoras again even though he supported Samos Rovers and they were knocked out in the first round of the Greek Islands league cup in 503 BC.

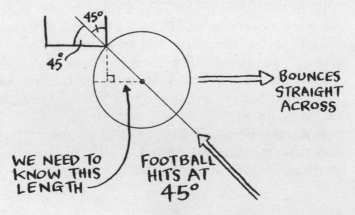

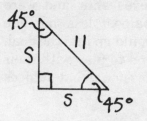

We can draw a little right-angled triangle. Because the two small angles are both 45°, the two short sides will be the same length. We know the long side is 11 cm. We'll call the short sides s.

Pythagoras says $s^2 + s^2 = 11^2$.
This turns into $2s^2 = 121$, so $s^2 = 121 \div 2 = 60\cdot5$

$$s = \sqrt{60\cdot5} = 7\cdot78 \text{ cm}$$

Now look at the diagram again. The target area for the ball to bounce on into the goal is $11 - 7\cdot78 = 3\cdot22$ cm.

The chances of the ball hitting the post and going on into the goal are:
<bounce-on target area> ÷ <total post target area>.

So that's $3\cdot22 \div 34 = 0\cdot095$ or about 9·5%.

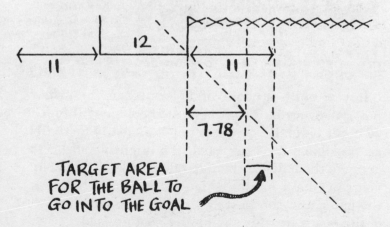

TARGET AREA FOR THE BALL TO GO INTO THE GOAL

Therefore if you had your eyes shut and were kicking the ball straight at a goalpost, less than one shot in ten that hits the post should go into the goal. This is why most footballers tend to play with their eyes open, which is very professional but it does rather spoil the fun.

How many footballs can you fit in a swimming pool?

Are you normal or nutty?
Here's your chance to find out if you're normal or if you're an utterly nutty Pure Mathematician. If you're normal, then you'll be able to read this next section without it driving you mad.

If you want to get as many balls as possible into the pool, it makes sense to arrange them in neat layers. These are the two best ways of doing it.

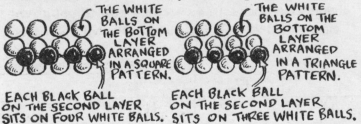

THE WHITE BALLS ON THE BOTTOM LAYER ARRANGED IN A SQUARE PATTERN.

THE WHITE BALLS ON THE BOTTOM LAYER ARRANGED IN A TRIANGLE PATTERN.

EACH BLACK BALL ON THE SECOND LAYER SITS ON FOUR WHITE BALLS.

EACH BLACK BALL ON THE SECOND LAYER SITS ON THREE WHITE BALLS.

If you built up lots of layers, then for either pattern, every ball that isn't at the edge will touch 12 other balls. If you want to get as many footballs as possible into your pool, it's slightly better to arrange the balls in the triangle pattern. Obviously you can't help having some empty space between the balls, and the best you can do is have about $\frac{1}{4}$ of the space in your swimming pool unused.

How did you get on?

If you are feeling happy and relaxed then you're normal. However utterly nutty people will now be driven MAD by two more questions.

1 Is it possible in any way to arrange the balls so that one ball can touch 13 other balls? This easy-looking question bothered Isaac Newton and other clever people for centuries, and it was only about 150 years ago that it was proved to be impossible.

2 If the balls are arranged in the triangular pattern, then the exact fraction of the space taken up in the pool is $\frac{\pi}{3\sqrt{2}} = 0\cdot74048$. But people think it might be possible to increase that fraction to a maximum of $0\cdot78$, if only somebody could find a better way of packing the balls. So if you see a bunch of Pure Mathematicians frolicking around in the ball pond at your local kids' play park, don't disturb them. It's important work.

Suppose your swimming pool is Olympic-sized, it would be 50 m × 25 m × 2 m. This gives a total volume of $50 \times 25 \times 2 = 2{,}500$ cubic metres. If you fill it with footballs, we know that about $\frac{1}{4}$ of the space can't be used, so the maximum volume of footballs will be $2{,}500 \times \frac{3}{4} = 1{,}875$ cubic metres. To see how many footballs we can fit in, we just need to divide this answer by the volume of a football. Seems simple enough doesn't it? Er, well...

How do you work out the volume of a football?

The most obvious way to work out the volume of a ball (or sphere) is to use the formula discovered by the ancient Greek genius Archimedes.

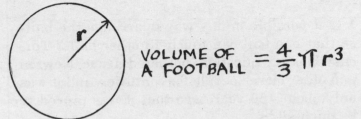

VOLUME OF A FOOTBALL $= \frac{4}{3}\pi r^3$

Unfortunately this formula is pretty useless when it comes to footballs because you need to know the radius. (That's the distance from the very middle of the football to the outside.) How are you supposed to measure that? If you've got an orange, you can cut it in half and then measure the radius, but if you cut a football in half it stops being a ball and just becomes a flat flappy thing. The only thing you can measure easily on a football is the circumference if you've got a tape measure. Once you know what that is, you've got a choice of two formulas to work out the volume.

The posh Sphere Volume from Circumference formula: Vol $= \frac{4\pi}{3}\left(\frac{c}{2\pi}\right)^3$	**What you have to do:** Divide the circumference by 2π (this gives you the radius r) then cube the answer to get r^3 and then multiply by π and then multiply by 4 then divide by 3... Ugh!

The super new Murderous Maths formula: $Vol = \frac{c^3}{60}$	**What you have to do:** Cube the circumference. Divide by 60. Eat a chocolate biscuit. Hooray!

The super new MM formula makes life much easier and gives a fairly accurate result. (If you want to be more accurate then divide your c^3 by 59·2176 instead of 60.)

If a football measures 680 mm in circumference, that's the same as 0·68 metres. The volume is $(0·68)^3 \div 60 = 0·00524$ cubic metres.

We already worked out that the maximum volume of footballs in an Olympic pool is 1,875 cubic metres, so the number of footballs you can get in the pool is:

1875 ÷ 0·00524 = 357,824 which is over a third of a million.

There's just one thing to watch out for. If you do fill a swimming pool with footballs, be sure to warn people before they dive in off the top board.

How can you measure the volume of a football?

Our Pure Mathematicians will demonstrate another way to find the volume of a football (or any other funny-shaped lumpy thing). You put it in a basin of water and hold it under the surface. Mark how far the water comes up the side of the basin.

Then take the ball out, and you'll find the water level drops. Get a measuring jug and use it to add more water until the level gets back to your mark.

The amount of water you add is the same as the volume of the ball. (1 litre of water = 0·001 cubic metres, so if you need 5·2 litres, this shows that the football volume is 0·0052 cubic metres.) This was another of Archimedes' brain waves, and he got the idea when he was in his bath about 2,250 years ago.

155

How much of Archimedes' bathwater is in every glass of water you drink?

Water is made up of billions of tiny little things called molecules. A water molecule has two atoms of hydrogen stuck to one atom of oxygen. There are about 33,500,000,000,000,000,000,000,000 molecules in 1 litre of water.

First we need to know how many water molecules there were in Archimedes' bath. We don't know what sort of bath Archimedes had but we'll look into it.

YOU'RE NOT LOOKING IN **MY** BATHWATER!

Oh. In that case we'll have to assume it's like a modern bath which holds about 200 litres. Therefore the number of water molecules in the bath is:

200 × the molecules in 1 litre. That comes to 6,700,000,000,000,000,000,000,000,000 molecules.

We now have to assume that in the last 2,000 years, these molecules have got into the sea and rivers, been evaporated by the sun, drifted along in clouds, came down in rain, got sucked up by plants and slurped up by animals, frozen into snowmen and have generally mixed in evenly with all the other water on the planet.

Our consultants in the Horrible Geography department tell us that the total amount of water on Earth is about 1,260,000,000,000,000,000,000 litres. We want to know how many bathwater molecules there are in each litre of water, so we simply divide the molecules by the litres:

$$\frac{6,700,000,000,000,000,000,000,000,000}{1,260,000,000,000,000,000,000} = 5,317,460$$

All drinks are mainly made of water, so for every litre you drink, you swallow over *five million* molecules of Archimedes' bath water.

Goodbye!

Sadly we're reached the end of this book, but for Murderous Maths fans the fun never finishes. If you want to find more freaky facts, strange tricks or mind-numbing numbers then we hope you'll join us at *www.murderousmaths.co.uk*.

In the meantime there's just one tiny little mystery left to clear up. As we've proved that giant people-eating spiders didn't exist, you might be wondering how the island got its name...

Place: Just passing Tiny Spider Island, Pacific Ocean
Date: 31 August 1929
Time: 12:30 pm

The seven men sat glumly in the back of the prison boat as it motored out across the sea. Standing over them was a man in a blue uniform with a big stick and a whistle.

"It still beats me why you wanted to get off that place," chortled Warden Collis. "If you hadn't put that kite up, we'd never have spotted you. You could have lived there for years."

"Never mind that," snapped Blade. "Just get us back into the prison. Is this Sharkfin Island coming up?"

The warden looked out at an island looming in front of them.

"No, that's Tiny Spider Island."

"Oh boy," muttered Half-Smile. "Why couldn't we have landed there? I ain't scared of tiny spiders."

"Ha ha," laughed the warden. "There ain't no tiny spiders on there. There's just beaches and fish pools and sunshine."

"So how does it get to be called Tiny Spider Island?"

"Because it's a tiny island! Oh, and the other part of its name is because it was discovered 200 years ago by Captain Sydney Spider. And the only island I know that's nicer than that one is a lot bigger and he discovered that one too. That why it's called…"

"GIANT SPIDER ISLAND!" groaned the seven men.

ISBN 978 1407 10714 1

ISBN 978 1407 10711 0

ISBN 978 1407 10713 4

ISBN 978 1407 10716 5